HARVEST OF FAITH

Paul H. D. Lang

Publishing House
St. Louis

COVER PHOTO: "Autumn Nest" by Alpha Photo: Hallinan, "Crocus in Snow" Alpha photo by Hallinan—14; "Trinity Lutheran Chaple, Cable, Wisconsin by Haertling—22; "The Forest and Yellow Wild Flowers" by Bruce Roberts—27; "Mountain Stream" alpha Photo by Hallinan—31; "Dogwood and Redbud in Bloom" Missouri Division of Commerce & Industrial Development—66; "Burch Trees" in Vermont" by Eastern Photo Co.—74; "Old Grist Mill in the Ozarks" by Jack Zehrt—82; "Crabapple Blossoms" by Louis Williams—90.

The Scripture quotations in this publication are from the Revised Standard Version Common Bible, copyrighted © 1973 by the Division of Christian Education of the National Council of the Churches of Christ in the U.S.A., and used by permission.

Concordia Publishing House, St. Louis, Missouri
Copyright © 1979 Concordia Publishing House

MANUFACTURED IN THE UNITED STATES OF AMERICA

Library of Congress Cataloging in Publication Data

Lang, Paul H D
    Harvest of faith.

    1. Aged—Prayer-books and devotions—English.
I. Title.
BV4580.L34   242'.6'5   78-13405
ISBN 0-570-03055-2

Contents

Preface

In my first book of devotions for the retired, *The Golden Days,* I mentioned that there were more than 20 million such citizens in the U.S.A. That number has now risen to over 25 million.

Threatened with idleness, uselessness, and fear of what lies ahead, many elderly are in need of guidance and support financially, physically, and emotionally. Fortunately our government and our communities are concerned about these needs and are doing much to alleviate them. But the elderly are above all in need of a right relationship with God through our Savior Jesus Christ. In order to be content and happy, they need to trust in God, to put themselves in His hands, to read and meditate on His Word, and to pray.

Life is happy and thrilling when we have something for which to live, not only for today and tomorrow but for eternity. The future is the ultimate purpose, the important goal. Happiness now and in the future comes from God. We are most happy when we trust in God's grace and love through Christ Jesus. Then we have forgiveness, peace, and hope. Life is worth living and hopeful when we pray and live every day in union with our gracious and loving God.

I thank all who have spoken and written to me expressing their appreciation for *The Golden Days*. I also thank my wife, Ann, for proofreading my manuscript.

May God bless this work and make it a blessing to all who use it.

Paul H. D. Lang

Does It Pay to Pray?

Ask, and it will be given you; seek, and you will find; knock, and it will be opened to you. For every one who asks receives, and he who seeks finds, and to him who knocks it will be opened. Or what man of you, if his son asks him for bread, will give him a stone? Or if he asks for a fish, will give him a serpent? If you then, who are evil, know how to give good gifts to your children, how much more will your Father who is in heaven give good things to those who ask Him!

Matt. 7:7-11 RSV

Our Lord directed and encouraged His followers to seek help, counsel, and every blessing in earnest prayer. Then He promised that everyone who asked, sought, and knocked would be successful in the request.

Of course, one could ask for something that God has not promised in His Word. Or one could offer proud and hypocritical prayers. Or one could pray while clinging to some sin or ask for things without the proper means of receiving them. A person could seek salvation in a way of his own devising, such as his good works, or pray in a fit of fear, ceasing to pray when the fear subsides.

If God announced that He would give money to everyone that should ask Him, how many would remain poor? Would not the gates of heaven be thronged perpetually with seekers for that gift? If honor and earthly success were promised for the asking, who would not ask for them? God can give these things, but He does not promise them.

However, God has promised sure success to everyone who comes as a poor sinner through Jesus Christ our Redeemer and Advocate—to everyone who seeks promised spiritual blessings or unpromised material blessings on the basis of "not my will, but Thine, be done." This promise is absolute. "Every one who asks receives, and he who seeks finds, and to him who knocks it will be opened." God does not go back on His promises. He is faithful, loving, kind, almighty, and compassionate. And since He has promised that all the glorious things of His divine grace and love are to be had simply for the asking, does it seem possible that any one should fail to ask? Who would give his hungry child that pleads for food a worthless stone instead of bread, or a serpent instead of fish? If, then, sinful and selfish human beings are by natural affections inclined to give good and useful gifts to their children, how much more will our heavenly Father give good things to everyone who humbly and believingly asks for them? Does it seem possible that anyone should fail to pray? The story is told about a man who died and was taken to heaven by an angel. Upon arriving he found a huge door with his name on it. Opening it, he entered a room filled with presents of all kinds. He eagerly asked the angel as to whether these were his, now that he had come to heaven. The angel answered, "No. These are the blessings that could have been yours on earth if only you had asked for them."

Christ directs and encourages also us senior citizens to pray and assures each one of us, "Ask, and it will be given you." Let us take Him at His word. We can pray any time and any place. Our participation in the church's worship is especially profitable. There Christ is present with us in His Word and Sacraments according to His promise, "Where two or three are gathered in My name, there am I in the midst of them." We can pray with our family at home in morning and evening devotions. We can speak to God freely and effectively by ourselves alone.

Let us not argue about why and how God can hear and answer our prayers. You never find a hungry child begin first to discuss the philosophical difficulties with his mother when he wants bread. You never find a person who really feels that he needs saving blessings pause to discuss how it is possible that God can answer prayer. The text that upsets all objections is, "Ask, and it will be given you." Does it pay to pray? Take God at His word and you will know that it does pay.

> When in the hour of utmost need
> We know not where to look for aid;
> When days and nights of anxious thought
> Nor help nor counsel yet have brought,
>
> Then this our comfort is alone,
> That we may meet before Thy throne
> And cry, O faithful God, to Thee
> For rescue from our misery;
>
> To Thee may raise our hearts and eyes,
> Repenting sore with bitter sighs,
> And seek Thy pardon for our sin
> And respite from our griefs within.
>
> For Thou has promised graciously
> To hear all those who cry to Thee
> Through Him whose name alone is great,
> Our Savior and our Advocate.
>
> And thus we come, O God, today
> And all our woes before Thee lay;
> For sorely tried, cast down, we stand,
> Perplexed by fears on every hand.
>
> Ah! hide not from our sins Thy face;
> Absolve us through Thy boundless grace,
> Be with us in our anguish still,
> Free us at last from every ill,
>
> That so with all our hearts we may
> To Thee our glad thanksgiving pay,
> Then walk obedient to Thy Word
> And now and ever praise Thee, Lord.

Sustained by Trust in God

In Thee, Lord, do I seek refuge; let me never be put to shame; in Thy righteousness deliver me! Incline Thy ear to me, rescue me speedily! Be Thou a rock of refuge for me, a strong fortress to save me! Yea, Thou art my Rock and my Fortress; for Thy name's sake lead me and guide me, take me out of the net which is hidden for me, for Thou art my Refuge. Into Thy hand I commit my spirit; Thou hast redeemed me, O Lord, faithful God. . . . My times are in Thy hand. . . . Be strong, and let your heart take courage, all you who wait for the Lord!

Ps. 31:1-5, 15, 24 RSV

This psalm expresses the prayer of one who is passing through a troubled period of life and is facing the prospect of death. In his great danger and trial he confidently expects deliverance from God.

Our Lord Jesus used the first words of verse 5 on the cross when he prayed to the Father, "Into Thy hands I commit my spirit."

If we trust in God for everything on the basis of His Word, He will not leave us disappointed in our hope. We will be sustained and inspired with confidence by the Holy Spirit. The Holy Spirit will also teach us what to say in our prayers.

God will not go back on His word. He will not leave us disappointed in our hope. His justice and mercy, based on the substitutionary suffering, death, and resurrection of His Son for our redemption, will move Him to forgive us our sins and rescue us from eternal condemnation. Our earnest prayers will draw down blessings from our reconciled Father as we stand in need of them. God will protect and support us when we flee to Him as our "Strong Fortress." He will build us up on the "rock" of our salvation. He will guide us in His holy way. He will free us from perplexities and deliver us from temptations. He will extricate us from the traps that Satan sets in our paths to destroy us.

We can look up to God in Christ, our Redeemer and Advocate, with the sure confidence that He will never leave us or forsake us. We can continually commit ourselves into His hands. In all our needs He sustains us. Even when death is near at hand, and when it actually comes, He will give us the ability to resign our spirit into His hand.

In the Manchester Art Gallery there is a famous picture entitled, "Into Thy Hands, O Lord." The picture represents a young knight clad in armor riding a white horse whose downcast head, quivering nostrils and limbs show intense fear. Behind the knight is a forest through which he had passed, but the path in front of him is full of gloom and unknown terrors. In his fear the knight is at one with the trembling horse. But he has within him that which raises him above the danger and sustains him. It is trust in God. Lifting his sword before his face, it forms itself into a cross. "Into Thy hands, O Lord," he says and goes forward. He conquers fear by faith. By it, though he walked "through the valley of the shadow of death," he feared no evil.

In Christ, God gives us a marvelous exchange. The exchange is between our sinfulness and Christ's righteousness. Christ took our sins and their consequences in His body and nailed them to the cross. Through faith in Him He gives us His perfect righteousness and eternal life. In His mercy He rescues us from condemnation and gives us pardon, peace, and eternal happiness. What a blessing!

Now, when we pray to our heavenly Father, Christ intercedes for us. The Father gives us His blessings as we stand in need of them. If we seek "refuge" in Him, we will "never be put to shame." His righteousness, credited to us, delivers us from sin, death, and condemnation. In our earthly troubles He is our "rock of refuge," "a strong fortress, to save." For His "name's sake" He will "lead . . . and guide" us.

Encouraged by the grace and loving-kindness of God in

Christ, let us cast all our cares on Him and commit our "spirit" into His hands. When we face enforced leisure, infirmities, and many other troubles of old age, let us cast our cares upon God. He will sustain us. Let us do what we can to solve the problems we face and make use of what others can do to help us, but for our peace and salvation let us trust in God alone. When we do that, He will sustain us and even make the last years of our life here on earth the best years.

In Thee, Lord, have I put my trust;
Leave me not helpless in the dust,
  Let me not be confounded,
Let in Thy Word my faith, O Lord,
  Be always firmly grounded.

Bow down Thy gracious ear to me
And hear my cries and prayers to Thee,
  Haste Thee for my protection;
For woes and fear surround me here.
  Help Me in my affliction.

My God and Shield, now let Thy power
Be unto me a mighty tower
  When bravely I defend me
Against the foes that round me close.
  O Lord, assistance lend me.

Thou art my Strength, my Shield, my Rock,
My Fortress that withstands each shock,
  My Help, my Life, my Treasure.
What'er the rod, Thou art my God;
  Naught can resist Thy pleasure.

With Thee, Lord, have I cast my lot;
O faithful God, forsake me not,
  To Thee my soul commending.
Lord, be my Stay, lead Thou the way
  Now and when life is ending.

All honor, praise, and majesty
To Father, Son and Spirit be,
  Our God forever glorious,
In whose rich grace we'll run our race
  Till we depart victorious.

"You Also Be Patient"

Be patient, therefore, brethren, until the coming of the Lord. Behold, the farmer waits for the precious fruit of the earth, being patient over it until it receives the early and the late rain. You also be patient. Establish your hearts, for the coming of the Lord is at hand. Do not grumble, brethren, against one another, that you may not be judged; behold, the Judge is standing at the doors. As an example of suffering and patience, brethren, take the prophets who spoke in the name of the Lord. Behold, we call those happy who were steadfast. You have heard of the steadfastness of Job, and you have seen the purpose of the Lord, how the Lord is compassionate and merciful.

James 5:7-11 RSV

Here St. James speaks to his poor, afflicted, persecuted, suffering, and disheartened fellow Christians. He exhorts them to bear their sufferings with patience, resignation, and constant perseverance until "the coming of the Lord." He refers them to the providential care of God in His coming to keep and comfort them in this life. But he also points forward to the hour of death and the final coming of Christ at the end of the world.

He asks them to look at a farmer. When a farmer has prepared his soil and sown the seed with great labor and expense, he cannot at once reap the harvest. What avails his haste? What avails his fretting? He may fret because a drought may come or there will be too much rain. But what does his fretting benefit him? Will his impatience change things? No; it can do no good. But patience can. He trusts in God. In quiet patience he waits for months while the weather fluctuates. He continually adds further labor in cultivating as necessary. He waits for the coming harvest season, sleeping and rising, rising and sleeping while the crop grows and while God, on whom he depends, sends "the early and the late rain." That is, he commits himself to the order of God. He has patience. He

13

goes on trusting that God in His own way will give him the harvest. Then at length the crop ripens and his work and waiting are amply rewarded by the harvest.

So we must look patiently to God in our retirement and old age. We must wait with patient hope and persevering diligence in prayer, worship, hobbies, and deeds of love and service. We must keep ourselves busy, preferably with creative and useful occupations. We must not yield to sloth, inactivity, weariness, discouragement, and despondency. But we must establish our hearts by faith in the promises of God. For the time of waiting is soon over, and the most glorious and precious harvest makes all our hardships, waitings, and sufferings worthwhile.

It is also inconsistent with our Christian faith to give way to envy of others, discontent, repining, or despondency. For the Judge, as it were, is already "standing at the door" to fulfill His promises. Let us prepare ourselves for His coming in providence and glory and leave it to Him to plead for us without our worrying about it. Let us persevere with calm confidence in God and submit ourselves to His will. Let us imitate the examples of the suffering and patience of the ancient prophets, such as Job, who persevered with confidence in God and committed themselves to His will with meekness and courage. Let us remember the apostles of Christ and other Christians, who were steadfast and even happy under persecution, infirmities, poverty, discouragements, and hardships in traveling from one country to another to preach the gospel. We shall find the same consolation and happiness in our troubles, provided we are patient and persevere in our faith in Christ, walking in His ways. All these prophets, apostles, and Christians experienced that their sufferings turned out for their spiritual and eternal advantage. So shall we.

Let us then be patient. For only when we keep ourselves

busy and remain patient and content can we be happy. Then the good seed we sow now in our weakness and sometimes water with tears, trusting in Christ, will spring up and ripen to a harvest of eternal glory and joy. Let us permit the Holy Spirit to establish our hearts with faith. For all our temporal and eternal happiness is secure when we trust in God and leave everything in His gracious and loving hands. Patience is a wonderful thing. Out of troubles it can draw peace, joy out of sorrow, comfort out of weakness. A person's troubles cannot make him despondent when he has patience. Even a poor beggar finds that patience can make him rich. "Behold, we call those happy who were steadfast" in faith and patience, and have learned "how the Lord is compassionate and merciful."

O God of Mercy, hear us;
  Our Father, be Thou near us;
Mid crosses and in sadness
  Be Thou our Fount of gladness.

To all who bow before Thee
  And for Thy grace implore Thee,
Oh, grant Thy benediction
  And patience in affliction.

Be Thou a Helper speedy
  To all the poor and needy,
To all forlorn a Father;
  Thine erring children gather.

Be with the sick and ailing,
  Their Comforter unfailing;
Dispelling grief and sadness,
  Oh, give them joy and gladness!

Above all else, Lord, send us
  Thy Spirit to attend us,
Within our hearts abiding,
  To heaven our footsteps guiding.

"Let Not Your Hearts Be Troubled"

"Let not your hearts be troubled; believe in God, believe also in Me. In My Father's house are many rooms; if it were not so, would I have told you that I go to prepare a place for you? And when I go and prepare a place for you, I will come again and will take you to Myself, that where I am you may be also. And you know the way where I am going." Thomas said to him, "Lord, we do not know where You are going; how can we know the way?" Jesus said to him, "I am the Way, and the Truth, and the Life; no one comes to the Father, but by Me."

John 14:1-6 RSV

Christ had told His disciples that He would go away from them. This troubled them. So He told them not to give way to anxiety, or despondency or to permit troubles to distress them. He reminded them of their belief in God. Likewise they should also believe in Him as the Son of God and the promised Messiah, the Savior. This faith would support them in their concerns and secure their happiness.

Then our Lord assured them that in His Father's house were many peaceful, enduring, and happy rooms prepared for them. He was about to go away from them to prepare a place in heaven for them. His going away was necessary for the atonement of their sins and the sins of all people. After His atoning death He would rise again. His resurrection would be the guarantee of their resurrection. He would therefore surely come again. He would at death receive their souls and on the last day raise them up, so that they might be forever with Him in that glorious and happy place to which He was going.

After all these instructions, our Lord took for granted that they knew the place where He was going and the way to it. But Thomas said, "Lord, we do not know where You are going; how can we know the way?" To this Christ answered, "I am the Way, and the Truth, and the Life; no one comes to the Father, but by Me."

Therefore Christ is our "Way" to the Father and to heaven. He is the Way in His person as God "manifested in the flesh," and as our Savior and Mediator by His perfect life and His atoning sacrifice on the cross. "He is the expiation for our sins, and not for ours only but also for the sins of the whole world." He is "the Truth," not only as God but also as the great Teacher whose doctrine is "the Way" to the Father and to Heaven. And he is "the Life" by whose life-giving Spirit the dead in sin are raised to spiritual life and brought to faith in Him. No one can approach God as Father who is not made spiritually alive through Jesus Christ as "the Life," is not instructed by Him as "the Truth," and does not come to Him as "the Way."

As we grow old we cannot help experiencing various forms of weakness, difficulties, troubles, sorrows, temptations, and sins. But as Christians we must guard against unbelief, despondency, worry, and despair. Faith in the promises of God and the grace and love of our Savior will help in our situation. It will procure inward peace, hope, and happiness. Even in the face of death we can live by the prospect of going to the glorious "rooms" in our Father's house. This hope will never disappoint us. The promises of Christ will never deceive us. He has told us that in this world we shall have tribulation. But He has gone to prepare a place for us. He is mindful of our concerns which we have now, and He will come again to take us to our heavenly home. Let us, therefore, diligently make use of His Word and Sacraments to uphold and prepare our souls for heaven and wait in patience and love for our final deliverance from all evil.

We do not know where heaven is. But the great fact that satisfies the heart is that Christ has gone there to prepare a place for us. Heaven is described for us in the Bible both negatively and positively. In heaven there is no more evil, no hunger and thirst, no sorrow, no more pain, no more death, no night, no things that destroy our present happiness, no ignorance, disease, selfishness, fear, doubt, and separation. Positively, heaven is a place of happiness, fullness of joy, glory, pleasure, peace, knowledge, music, worship; a place of things that eyes have not seen, ears have not heard, nor have ever entered into human hearts. It is a life with God, who is the fountain of happiness. It is eternal. It will not fade away but continue when time shall be no more, lasting forever.

How do we get to heaven? Most people entertain the idea of going to heaven. They have some hope of life after death. They want to go to heaven. But wanting to go is not enough. Christ has told us the "way" to heaven. He said, "I am the Way, and the Truth, and the Life: no one comes to the Father, but by Me." By the grace of God let us then go that "Way," learn and believe that "truth," live in and with that "Life" by trusting in and confessing Jesus Christ. In that way we shall go to our Father's house, into the glorious place to which our Lord and Savior has gone to prepare a "place" for us.

> On Christ's ascension I now build
>   The hope of my ascension;
> This hope alone has ever stilled
>   All doubt and apprehension;
> For where the Head is, there full well
> I know His members are to dwell
>   When Christ shall come and call them.
> Since He returned to claim His throne,
>   Great gifts for men obtaining,
> My heart shall rest in Him alone,
>   No other rest remaining;
> For where my Treasure went before,
> There all my thoughts shall ever soar
>   To still their deepest yearning.
> Oh, grant, dear Lord, this grace to me,
>   Recalling Thine ascension,
> That I may ever walk with Thee,
>   Adorning Thy redemption;
> And then, when all my days shall cease,
> Let me depart in joy and peace
>   In answer to my pleading.

"The Lord Is My Shepherd"

The Lord is my shepherd, I shall not want; He makes me lie down in green pastures. He leads me beside still waters; He restores my soul. He leads me in paths of righteousness for His name's sake. Even though I walk through the valley of the shadow of death, I fear no evil; for Thou art with me; Thy rod and Thy staff, they comfort me. Thou preparest a table before me in the presence of my enemies; Thou anointest my head with oil, my cup overflows. Surely goodness and mercy shall follow me all the days of my life; and I shall dwell in the house of the Lord for ever.

Ps. 23 RSV

Here the psalmist speaks in simple words and figures of God's love for us and our trust in Him.

The picture of the shepherd and his sheep is not only beautiful but most meaningful for us. A shepherd loves his sheep. They are his pride and joy. It is his one concern to take good care of them. He is with them day and night. He provides for them good food and drink. When they are in danger he protects them. He will even lay down his life for the sheep, as Christ says in John 10:11. In saying this, He was applying the picture of the shepherd and his sheep to Himself. If an ordinary shepherd has such devotion for his sheep, how is it possible for us to lack any good thing when Christ, the almighty, ever-present and all-wise Son of God is our Good Shepherd? He does not always give us what we want or what we think is good for us, but that is because we do not always know what is best for us. But God knows. He gives us what we should have. If we would always believe that the Lord is our shepherd, we shall not want, would we ever be anxious and worry? No. We would have peace and happiness of the kind that the unbelievers do not have and cannot know.

What can we want, when we have Christ for our Good Shepherd? What will our Savior withhold from us, for whom He shed His blood on the cross for the forgiveness of our sins and to give us eternal life and salvation? Will not He who redeemed our souls from death provide for our bodies? Surely our worries and frustrations come from our lack of faith. Let us then make use of the means of grace, God's Word and Sacraments, for the strengthening of our faith. Let us drink of the "still waters" of salvation and simply trust in our Shepherd's care.

The psalmist does not speak about Christ and His sheep in general terms. He says, "the Lord is My Shepherd . . . He leads me." He uses the personal pronoun "I" 4 times; "He" 4 times; "me" 7 times; "my" 5 times. It is not enough for us to learn of God's grace and loving-kindness towards the world in general, for example, "The Lord is gracious and merciful, slow to anger and abounding in steadfast love" (Ps. 103:8). We need and long for a personal assurance that God loves "me" and takes care of "me." Our Lord assures us of this in John 10, where he says, "the sheep hear His voice, and He calls His own sheep by name." God loves you and me, He watches over you and me, He takes care of you and me, He has redeemed you and me from sin, death, and damnation.

The psalmist says, "Thy rod and Thy staff, they comfort me." A shepherd uses his rod and staff both to protect and to guide his sheep. When attacked by a wolf he defends his sheep with his rod and staff. When a sheep goes astray, he uses his rod and staff to guide it in the right way. So Christ protects, as well as guides us. He chastens as well as blesses, and all this for our temporal and eternal good.

What does "goodness and mercy shall follow me all the days of my life" mean? Why "follow"? We realize our blessings only as we look back. We have experienced forgiveness of sins, life, and salvation, as well as sunshine, the joy of work, family, and friends. These experiences are a guarantee of present and future "goodness and mercy." We walk by faith—

faith in the Word and promises of God and the blessings we have had, now have, and will have.

Yes, "will have," in heaven after death. "I shall dwell in the house of the Lord for ever." The Good Shepherd will receive us into the "rooms" (John 14:2 RSV) that He, as our Good Shepherd, has gone to prepare for us. Let us thank and worship Him for the "goodness and mercy" by which He incorporated us into His family. In the end we shall dwell in the house of the Lord forever, where there is fullness of joy and where there are pleasures for evermore.

> The King of Love my Shepherd is,
>   Whose goodness faileth never;
> I nothing lack if I am His
>   And He is mine forever.
>
> Where streams of living water flow,
>   My ransomed soul He leadeth,
> And where the verdant pastures grow,
>   With food celestial feedeth.
>
> Perverse and foolish oft I strayed,
>   But yet in love He sought me
> And on his shoulder gently laid
>   And home, rejoicing, brought me.
>
> In death's dark vale I fear no ill,
>   With Thee, dear Lord, beside me;
> Thy rod and staff my comfort still,
>   Thy cross before to guide me.
>
> Thou spread'st a table in my sight,
>   Thy unction grace bestoweth;
> And, oh! the transport of delight
>   With which my cup o'erfloweth.
>
> And so through all the length of days
>   Thy goodness faileth never.
> Good Shepherd, may I sing Thy praise
>   Within Thy house forever!

A Sure Faith

Preserve Me, O God, for in Thee I take refuge. I say to the Lord, "Thou art My Lord; I have no good apart from Thee." As for the saints in the land, they are the noble, in whom is all My delight. Those who choose another god multiply their sorrows; their libations of blood I will not pour out or take their names upon My lips. The Lord is My chosen portion and My cup; Thou holdest my lot. The lines have fallen for Me in pleasant places; yea, I have a goodly heritage. I bless the Lord, who gives Me counsel; in the night also My heart instructs Me. I keep the Lord always before Me; because He is at My right hand, I shall not be moved. Therefore My heart is glad, and My soul rejoices; My body also dwells secure. For Thou dost not give Me up to Sheol, or let Thy godly One see the Pit. Thou dost show Me the path of life; in Thy presence there is fullness of joy, in Thy right hand are pleasures for evermore.

Ps. 16 RSV

During this writer's ministry, a number of people expressed their philosophy of life by saying, "I was born, I live, I shall die, and that is all there is to it." That is all there is to it. How tragic.

An article about the manufacture of cars describes a popular and high-priced car that had so and so much horse power. He said that one could drive it as fast as he desired. "But," he said, "the only trouble is that most people, when they get to the point in life when they can afford to buy this car, they are so old that they do not care to drive over 40 to 50 miles an hour."

That is what happens to many persons. They spend their lives trying to make as much money as possible and then they have lost the ability to enjoy what they have accumulated. There are many such tragedies in life. But there is no greater and more pitiful tragedy than for a person to live so as to miss the real point of life. Then when old age comes and death has to be faced, there is no sure faith by which to look forward to a

24

happy retirement and an eternity of perfect peace and joy in heaven.

In Psalm 16 Christ, the Messiah, speaks through David and says to His heavenly Father: "Thou dost not give Me up to Sheol, or let Thy godly One see the Pit." Peter quotes these words in his sermon on Pentecost Day as a prophecy of Christ's resurrection.

David himself looked forward to the Messiah. He was sure that the Son of God would come to redeem him from sin, death, and hell by His life, death, and resurrection. It was this that filled him with faith, hope, and happiness. It was this that enabled him to live with confidence and look forward with peace and joy.

If we had only ourselves and the things of this world to turn to, life would be miserable and hopeless. But we have a Savior, Jesus Christ. He lived, died, rose again, and ascended into heaven for us and our salvation. We have His own words for it, and Paul exclaims: "What then shall we say to this? If God is for us, who is against us? He who did not spare His own Son but gave Him up for us all, will He not also give us all things with Him? Who shall bring any charge against God's elect? It is God who justifies; who is to condemn? Is it Christ Jesus, who died, yes, who was raised from the dead, who is at the right hand of God, who indeed intercedes for us? Who shall separate us from the love of Christ? Shall tribulation, or distress, or persecution, or famine, or nakedness, or peril, or sword? . . . No, in all these things we are more than conquerors through Him who loved us. For I am sure that neither death, nor life, nor angels, nor principalities, nor things present, nor things to come, nor powers, nor height, nor depth, nor anything else in all creation, will be able to separate us from the love of God in Christ Jesus our Lord" (Rom. 8:31-35, 37-39 RSV).

This has a special meaning for us in our old age. We know

that life rushes on. We cannot escape death and the Judgment to come. In the face of this, how wonderful it is to have a faith and hope to live by in the person of Christ, our Lord and Savior In that faith and hope we can live victoriously. We can look up to God and say, "In Thy presence there is fullness of joy, in Thy right hand are pleasures for evermore." With that faith and hope to live by, we can face with confidence whatever still confronts us in our lives today. There is a God who loves us. There is a Savior who has redeemed us from sin, death, and damnation. Paul said, "I consider that the sufferings of this present time are not worth comparing with the glory that is to be revealed to us" (Rom. 8:18 RSV). So we can go on. We can leave to our God of love to work out for us whatever happens from day to day.

How can we have such a philosophy, such a faith and hope, by which to live? How can we be strengthened and sustained in it? The answer is: by letting God give it to us. He comes to us in His Word and Sacraments. He listens to us in our prayers. Therefore, let us live confidently, happily, surely, and hopefully and say: "In Thy presence there is fullness of joy, in Thy right hand are pleasures for evermore."

> I know my faith is founded
>   On Jesus Christ, my God and Lord;
> And this my faith confessing,
>   Unmoved I stand upon His Word.
> Man's reason cannot fathom
>   The truth of God profound;
> Who trusts her subtle wisdom
>   Relies on shifting ground.
> God's Word is all-sufficient,
>   It makes divinely sure,
> And, trusting in its wisdom,
>   My faith shall rest secure.
> Increase my faith, dear Savior,
>   For Satan seeks by night and day
> To rob me of this treasure
>   And take my hope of bliss away.
> But, Lord, with Thee beside me,

I shall be undismayed;
And led by Thy good Spirit,
   I shall be unafraid.
Abide with me, O Savior,
   A firmer faith bestow;
Then I shall bid defiance
   To every evil foe.

In faith, Lord, let me serve Thee;
   Though persecution, grief, and pain
Should seek to overwhelm me,
   Let me a steadfast trust retain;
And then at my departure
   Take Thou me home to Thee
And let me there inherit
   All Thou hast promised me.
In life and death, Lord, keep me
   Until Thy heaven I gain,
Where I by Thy great mercy
   The end of faith attain.

Things That Abide Forever

Do not love the world or the things in the world. If any one loves the world, love for the Father is not in him. For all that is in the world, the lust of the flesh and the lust of the eyes and the pride of life, is not of the Father but is of the world. And the world passes away, and the lust of it; but he who does the will of God abides for ever.

1 John 2:15-17 RSV

When St. John wrote these words, he was an old man, probably nearly 100 years old. The people he addressed had all received one great blessing. They were Christians. Their sins were forgiven. They were God's children. This was something that made them happy. It had taken away worry and fear. It had given them courage, hope, peace, and joy. Some of these Christians were old. Their years of experience in life had given them a fuller, richer knowledge of worldly things and of the blessings of the Christian life. That is also true of us retirees. We have more experience than younger people. We know life better. As Christians we know God better. Some persons feel that old people should get out of the affairs of the world and the church and let the young people take charge. But that is not true. As long as the old people are physically and mentally capable, they are the greatest asset to society and the church. For they have the experience, knowledge, wisdom, and dignity necessary for the guidance of youth.

God has put us into the world, and as long as we are in it we have an obligation to do what we can for its welfare and benefit. For this is God's world. He made it. He keeps it. It is beautiful and wonderful. It reveals to us the power and wisdom of God. But God does not want us to put the world in place of Himself. Those who say they do not read the Bible or go to church but worship nature are deceiving themselves. St. John

29

says, "Do not love the world or the things in the world." By this he means that we are not to love the evil things in the world or to be so much attached to this world that we are indifferent to God who made the world. The world and the things of the world are not the end in themselves but the means to the end. They should lead us to God, not away from Him. We are not to love the unbelieving, godless world and the way of unbelievers and wicked people. We are not to love "the lust of the eyes and the pride of life."

"The world passes away, and the lust of it." If a person has gained all the world can give in wealth, distinction, and honor but has nothing else, what has he gained? Not long ago a man in the prime of life, the heir of millions of dollars, living in a million dollar palace, was shot down by an employee. If he had nothing but these worldly possessions, what has he now? Some years ago the Russian czar had unlimited power and resources. He owned many palaces. What has he now? "The world passes away, and the lust of it." Money and things that money can buy may be convenient, but "you cannot take them with you." If you put your heart on these things, you will be bitterly disappointed.

But St. John does not only tell us what we are not to do. He also tells us what we are to do. He tells us that there is One whom we should love. Instead of loving things, we should love Him who made all things. If we do this, then we have a heavenly Father, a Savior, and the Holy Spirit of God. That is the all-important thing in life. Sometimes we find ourselves bereaved of our loved ones and friends. We have been retired and don't know what to do. But when we have God and love Him, then we have a Father who loves us and is interested in our welfare and happiness. He gives us faith, peace, and joy in the forgiveness of sins and the sure hope of eternal life. That is why St. John says, "Do not love the world" but love God.

If we trust in God and love Him we will never be

lonesome, discouraged, or disappointed. We can always look upward. As each day goes by and we keep ourselves busy with things we can do and like to do, if we devote ourselves to the service of God and people, the closer we come to the place in heaven that Christ has gone to prepare for us, the better off we are. "The world passes away, and the lust of it; but he who does the will of God abides for ever."

What is the world to me
  With all its vaunted pleasure
When Thou, and Thou alone,
  Lord Jesus, art my Treasure!
Thou only, dearest Lord,
  My soul's Delight shall be;
Thou art my Peace, my Rest—
  What is the world to me!

The world is like a cloud
  And like a vapor fleeting,
A shadow that declines,
  Swift to its end retreating.
My Jesus doth abide,
  Though all things fade and flee;
My everlasting Rock—
  What is the world to me!

The world seeks to be praised
  And honored by the mighty,
Yet never once reflects
  That they are frail and flighty.
But what I truly prize
  Above all things is He,
My Jesus, He alone—
  What is the world to me!

The world with its wanton pride
  Exalts its sinful pleasures
And for them foolishly
  Gives up the heavenly treasures.
Let others love the world
  With all its vanity;
I love the Lord, my God—
What is the world to me.

The world abideth not;
  Lo, like a flash 'twill vanish;

With all its gorgeous pomp
    Pale death it cannot banish;
Its riches pass away,
    And all its joys must flee;
But Jesus doth abide—
    What is the world to me!

What is the world to me!
    My Jesus is my Treasure,
My Life, my Health, my Wealth,
    My Friend, my Love, my Pleasure,
My Joy, my Crown, my All,
    My Bliss eternally.
Once more, then, I declare:
    What is the world to me!

Trust in God's Promises

By faith Abraham obeyed when he was called to go out to a place which he was to receive as an inheritance; and he went out not knowing where he was to go. By faith he sojourned in the land of promise, as in a foreign land, living in tents with Isaac and Jacob, heirs with him of the same promise. For he looked forward to the city which has foundations, whose builder and maker is God. By faith Sarah herself received power to conceive, even when she was passed the age, since she considered Him faithful who had promised. Therefore from one man, and him as good as dead, were born descendants as many as the stars of heaven and as the innumerable grains of sand by the seashore. These all died in faith, not having received what was promised, but having seen it and greeted it from afar, and having acknowledged that they were strangers and exiles on the earth. For people who speak thus make it clear that they are seeking a homeland. If they had been thinking of that land from which they had gone out, they would have had opportunity to return. But as it is, they desire a better country, that is, a heavenly one. Therefore God is not ashamed to be called their God, for he has prepared for them a city.

Heb. 11:8-16 RSV

Abraham, Sarah, Isaac, and Jacob continued in the faith even unto death. They trusted in God's promises, "not having received what was promised," either the inheritance of Canaan or the coming of the Messiah, the Christ, during their lifetime. They experienced many hardships and trials. But they had faith. "Having seen it (the promised blessing) and greeted it from afar" they were sure that it would be fulfilled in due time to their posterity. For its sake they gave up their present advantages and "acknowledged that they were strangers and exiles on the earth." If they had not trusted in the promise, "they would have had opportunity to return" to their homeland. But that would have been an act of unbelief. By continuing to go on in a strange land until they died, they expressed their hope and desire for a better country than could be found on earth, even "a heavenly one," which

Canaan typified. Therefore they were willing to renounce all other prospects for the sake of following God in obedient faith. They looked forward to an eternal and invisible inheritance, a permanent, glorious city. Therefore God was "not ashamed to be called their God," their Friend and everlasting Savior.

One day we too will also be called to leave our worldly connections for a future inheritance. If we have Abraham's faith, we shall go on with confidence and hope. We shall not be satisfied with this world but "desire a better country, that is, a heavenly one." It is true, our faith is not always as strong as it should be. Yet, considering Him faithful, who has promised, we shall be strengthened through God's Word and Sacraments. If we acknowledge that we are "strangers and exiles on the earth," we shall look forward to the home where our treasure and heart already are. There Christ has gone to prepare a place for us, a "city" of His special abode, in which He will make us most happy and blessed for ever. Let us stake our life on this promise. Let us live by it and die by it. While we are here, our faith must be tried repeatedly, but we can be sure that we shall be strengthened in proportion to the trials. We remember that when Abraham was tried, he was willing to sacrifice his beloved son Isaac, but God did not let it happen. Let us then trust in God's promises and be willing to make lesser sacrifices as they come to us in our old age. The Lord will make up all our losses. He will even bless us by means of our disabilities, aches and pains, loneliness, and other trials.

An elderly person once said to this writer, "Let the perishable go, the inheritance is mine." Like that person, be indifferent to what the world gives or withholds. Life is not, as the world thinks, composed of wealth, health, honor, and abiding pleasure. It is the inner spiritual life in Christ that assures us of God's grace and love—a pure heart, a peaceful conscience, and inner happiness, a joyful hope, and eternal fellowship and communion with God for ever. This promise is sure. "He who did not spare His own Son but gave Him up for us all, will He not also give us all things with Him?" (Rom. 8:32 RSV).

A pilgrim and a stranger,
   I journey here below;
Far distant is my country,
   The home to which I go.
Here I must toil and travel,
   Oft weary and opprest;
But there my God shall lead me
   To everlasting rest.

I've met with storms and danger
   E'en from my early years,
With enemies and conflicts,
   With fightings and with fears.
There's nothing here that tempts me
   To wish a longer stay,
So I must hasten forward,
   No halting or delay.

It is a well-worn pathway;
   A host has gone before,
The holy saints and prophets,
   The patriarchs of yore.
They trod the toilsome journey
   In patience and in faith;
And them I fain would follow,
   Like them in life and death.

Who would share Abraham's blessing
   Must Abraham's path pursue,
A stranger and a pilgrim,
   Like him, must journey through.
The foes must be encountered,
   The dangers must be passed;
A faithful soldier only
   Receives the crown at last.

So I must hasten forward—
   Thank God the end will come!
The land of passing shadows
   Is not my destined home.
The everlasting city,
   Jerusalem above,

This evermore abideth,
  The home of light and love.
There I shall dwell forever,
  No more a parting guest,
With all Thy blood-bought children
  In everlasting rest.
The pilgrim toils forgotten,
  The pilgrim conflicts o'er,
All earthly griefs behind me,
  Eternal joys before.

"Cast Your Burden on the Lord"

Cast your burden on the Lord, and He will sustain you.

Humble yourselves therefore under the mighty hand of God, that in due time He may exalt you. Cast all your anxieties on Him, for He cares about you. Be sober, be watchful. Your adversary the devil prowls around like a roaring lion, seeking someone to devour. Resist him, firm in your faith, knowing that the same experience of suffering is required of your brotherhood throughout the world. And after you have suffered a little while, the God of all grace, who has called you to His eternal glory in Christ, will Himself restore, establish, and strengthen you. To Him be dominion for ever and ever. Amen.

Ps. 55:22; 1 Peter 5:6-11 RSV

Here the psalmist exhorts us to cast on God whatever burden he has allotted us, and to commit it to Him by faith and prayer. This is how we will find peace and happiness.

Likewise St. Peter tells us to cast all our anxieties humbly on God, for He cares about us. Humility is required, because God is against all proud and self-righteous persons. He shows favor only to those who realize their sinfulness and unworthiness. He confers grace and mercy only on those who are penitent and long for forgiveness for the sake of Christ, the Redeemer and Savior of the world.

Let us therefore humble ourselves under the mighty hand of God, who is able to crush His proud enemies and to uphold His penitent friends. By submitting ourselves to the righteousness of Christ, we are reconciled to God, and in due time He will exalt us to the glory and immortality prepared for all who believe. In the meantime, let us cast our burdens on the Lord, and He will sustain us.

This applies especially to us who are afflicted with the various difficulties, disabilities, and problems of old age. We need to commit ourselves fully into the hands of God, assured that He will manage everything to our advantage according to His wisdom and unfailing love.

The apostle exhorts us to watchfulness, since the devil makes use of every opportunity to destroy us. We must therefore keep ourselves busy with whatever we can and like to do. For "idleness is the devil's workshop." We must resist him by firmness of faith in Christ, depending on the power of God to drive him away. The apostle reminds us that our fellow Christians have the same experience of suffering that we have. St. Peter himself had the same experience when he was unwatchful. Then the devil induced him to deny his Lord and Savior three times with an oath. But when he repented with bitter tears, the Lord graciously sustained him and forgave him his sins.

As we grow old we sometimes feel weary and heavy laden. How shall we understand this? We should recognize that our life here is our time of training and preparation for eternal rest and glory. If we neglect this, if we carry our burdens only because we must, if we grumble and complain all the time, we will not benefit from our burden-bearing. But if we accept the fact that our burdens are a blessing in disguise and make cheerful use of them as our religious training, we shall find that "This slight momentary affliction is preparing for us an eternal weight of glory beyond all comparison" (2 Cor. 4:17 RSV).

How wonderful these exhortations are! "Cast your burden on the Lord." "Cast all your anxieties on Him, for He cares about you." Someone gave this illustration about the folly of those who do not trust Christ to bear their burdens for them: "Yonder is a train. A traveler comes to it dragging a heavy trunk. He sees the baggage car. In the door of that car stands a baggageman, who says, 'Bring your trunk here and I will take care of it for you.' But the traveler shakes his head. The train is about to start. He gets on the platform, drawing his trunk up so that it rests partly on the step of the car, but must be held all the time or it will slip off and be lost. And there, as the train moves on, stands the man holding himself by the railing on the platform with one hand and his trunk with the other, sighing and grumbling all the way. His trunk ought to be in the baggage car, being taken care of by the baggageman. The man should be comfortable, seated in the passenger car. There is no need for him to be on the platform, holding his trunk. That passenger I never saw and never expect to see. But I have seen Christians just like him— Christians who insist on being miserable when God has made the most ample provisions for their comfort, help, and happiness."

How about casting our burdens on the Lord? He is our Burden-bearer, the divine Helper, who cares for us as tenderly as a mother for her baby. When we cast our burdens on Him, He takes care of them and transforms them into blessings for us now and for ever.

If thou but suffer God to guide thee
  And hope in Him through all thy ways,
He'll give thee strength, whate'er betide thee,
  And bear thee through the evil days.
Who trusts in God's unchanging love
  Builds on the Rock that naught can move.

What can these anxious cares avail thee,
  These never-ceasing moans and sighs?
What can it help if thou bewail thee
  O'er each dark moment as it flies?
Our cross and trials do but press
  The heavier for our bitterness.

Don't think amid the fiery trial
  That God hath cast thee off unheard,
That he whose hopes meet no denial
  Must surely be of God preferred.
Time passes and much change doth bring
  And sets a bound to everything.

Sing, pray, and keep His ways unswerving,
  Perform thy duties faithfully,
And trust His Word, though undeserving,
  Thou yet shalt find it true for thee.
God never yet forsook in need
  The soul that trusted Him indeed.

Trust in the Lord and Enjoy Security

Trust in the Lord, and do good; so you will dwell in the land, and enjoy security. . . . Commit your way to the Lord; trust in Him, and He will act. . . . Be still before the Lord, and wait patiently for Him; fret not yourself over him who prospers in his way, over the man who carries out evil devices. . . . The salvation of the righteous is from the Lord; He is their refuge in the time of trouble. The Lord helps them and delivers them; He delivers them from the wicked, and saves them, because they take refuge in Him.

Ps. 37:3, 5, 7, 39-40 RSV

On one of his trips for the study of animals and plants, Charles Darwin found in the Pacific Ocean a plant that rose from the depth of 150 to 200 feet and floated on the great breakers of the ocean. The stem of this plant was less than an inch thick. Yet it held its own against the fierce smitings and pressures of the breakers. What was the secret of its marvelous strength and endurance? The answer is that its roots were fastened so firmly in the rocks at the bottom of the ocean that no commotion of the waters could shake it loose.

When we "trust in the Lord," when the roots of faith are fastened to Jesus Christ, we "enjoy security." No surface agitations and pressures in life can overcome us. There may be times in our old age when our inner and outer experiences are rough, painful, and discouraging, but we shall survive it all and preserve our integrity, happiness, and hope by the grace and power of God.

Psalm 37 was probably written by David when he was an old man. He wrote it by divine inspiration and as the result of his long experience and observation of life No doubt he wrote it also for the instruction and encouragement of his people, in case they would pass through such trying circumstances as he had experienced. But as far as we are concerned, it is the Word of God and has been written for us, that "by steadfastness and by the encouragement of the scriptures we might have hope" (Rom. 15:4 RSV).

The psalm refers to the present and future condition of the godly and the ungodly persons. This is of the greatest importance to us, because it shows us what to choose and to expect. We are not to be deceived by outward appearances. As we look around, it may seem to us sometimes that the ungodly prosper, flourish, and enjoy happiness, while the godly persons suffer all kinds of troubles, pain, and sorrow. But the flourishing of the ungodly is like the grass that is soon cut down and withered. Soon they will be no more on earth. Heaven they cannot enter. Hell alone remains for them. But the godly, those who believe in Christ and are covered by the righteousness of Christ, have other supports and will come to a blessed end. They "trust in the Lord and do good." They commit their ways to the Lord, trust in Him, and expect their happiness from Him. Their salvation is from the Lord. "He is their refuge in time of trouble."

Yes, we Christians have tribulations in the world. We are not exempt from the common afflictions of life and old age. In addition to these we are in fact afflicted with greater troubles, such as being hated and persecuted by the ungodly. But these passing sorrows are only a part of our Christian training and are not worth worrying about. All our temporal and eternal interests are in the Lord's hands. He loves us with an exceedingly great love. He is with us to strengthen and comfort us. What is more, He who has made us spiritually alive in Christ will raise us to eternal life with Himself in heaven. Life here and hereafter is all one. It begins here and is completed hereafter. We live now in and with Christ. Finally when Christ comes again He will receive us into our heavenly home, there to be with Him in perfect bliss and happiness for ever. Let us keep this goal before us and be comforted and cheered by its promises. God will never leave us or forsake us. As we trust in Christ and live according to His will now, we have nothing to worry about for the future or the present. He is our Friend and Companion in our lonesomeness and all our other troubles. In and with Him we now enjoy security and the future will also be taken care of by God.

Commit whatever grieves thee
  Into the gracious hands
Of Him who never leaves thee.
  Who heaven and earth commands.
Who points the clouds their courses,
  Whom winds and waves obey,
He will direct thy footsteps
  And find for thee a way.

On Him place thy reliance
  If thou wouldst be secure;
His work thou must consider
  If thine is to endure.
By anxious signs and grieving
  And self-tormenting care
God is not moved to giving;
  All must be gained by prayer.

Leave all to His direction;
  In wisdom He doth reign,
And in a way most wondrous
  His course He will maintain.
Soon He, His promise keeping,
  With wonder-working skill,
Shall put away the sorrows
  That now thy spirit fill.

Oh faithful child of heaven,
  How blessed shalt thou be!
With songs of glad thanksgiving
  A crown awaiteth thee.
Into thy hand thy Maker
  Will give the victor's palm,
And thou to thy Deliverer
  Shall sing a joyous psalm.

"Jesus, Lover of My Soul"

Praise the Lord! Praise the Lord, O my soul! I will praise the Lord as long as I live; I will sing praises to my God while I have being. Put not your trust in princes, in a son of man, in whom there is no help. When his breath departs he returns to his earth; on that very day his plans perish. Happy is he whose help is the God of Jacob, whose hope is in the Lord his God, who made heaven and earth, the sea, and all that is in them; who keeps faith for ever; who executes justice for the oppressed; who gives food to the hungry. The Lord sets the prisoners free; the Lord opens the eyes of the blind. The Lord lifts up those who are bowed down; the Lord loves the righteous. The Lord watches over the sojourners, He upholds the widow and the fatherless; but the way of the wicked he brings to ruin. The Lord will reign for ever, thy God, O Zion, to all generations. Praise the Lord!

Ps. 146 RSV

This psalm begins and ends with "Praise the Lord!" It was probably written by King David near the end of his reign and life. Isaac Watts expressed its meaning when he wrote:

I'll praise my Maker whilst I've breath;
And when my voice is lost in death,
    Praise shall employ my noble powers.
My days of praise shall ne'er be past,
While life and thought and being last,
    And immortality endures.

All the angels and saints in heaven sing "Praise the Lord!" Also the believers in Christ on earth are often so raised above their fears, sorrows and troubles that they join in the song of the angels and saints. Happy is the person who has the God of Jacob for his Savior, "whose hope is in the Lord his God, who made heaven and earth, the sea, and all that is in them." Such a person cannot help praising Him for His grace and loving kindness in providence and, above all, in redeeming us lost and condemned sinners. He proved His love and faithfulness to His Word by giving His Son to be our Savior. The Son of God and Man is not without power, as princes and the sons of man are. He is the almighty God who brings help and eternal salvation to all who trust in Him. Through His death on the cross and His glorious resurrection He redeemed us from sin, death, and hell. He lives and reigns for ever. When we trust in Him, our faith and hope rest on "the God of Jacob." When He was visibly on earth He freed those who were oppressed, He gave food to the hungry, He opened the eyes of the blind, He healed those who were diseased, He raised the dead, and He showed Himself the Friend of the widow and the destitute. But all this was only the example and sign of what He is doing today. He gives understanding to those who are spiritually ignorant, He raises those who are bowed down with a guilty conscience or by great distress, He feeds those who are hungry with the Bread of Life, and He is the constant Friend of the "poor in spirit" (Matt. 5:3), the destitute, and the helpless. He is the Comforter of those that mourn and are despondent.

All this has a special meaning for us in our old age. Christ is our Physician and Helper in every situation. Let us then flee to Him in our needs of soul and body. He loves us and will take care of us now and for ever. Let us trust Him for everything. Let us rejoice in Him as our gracious and loving Friend and Savior. Let us encourage one another, without ceasing, to praise His holy name and sing, "Praise the Lord! Praise the Lord, O my soul! I will praise the Lord as long as I live; I will sing praises to my God while I have being . . . Praise the Lord!"

> Jesus, Lover of my soul,
>   Let me to Thy bosom fly
> While the nearer waters roll,
>   While the tempest still is high.
> Hide me, O my Savior, hide,
>   Till the storm of life is past;
> Safe into the haven guide.
>   Oh, receive my soul at last!

Other refuge have I none;
   Hangs my helpless soul on Thee.
Leave, ah, leave me not alone,
   Still support and comfort me!
All my trust on Thee is stayed,
   All my help from Thee I bring;
Cover my defenseless head
   With the shadow of Thy wing.

Wilt Thou not regard my call,
   Wilt Thou not accept my prayer?
Lo, I sin, I faint, I fall;
   Lo, on Thee I cast my care;
Reach me out Thy gracious hand!
   While I of Thy strength receive,
Hoping against hope, I stand,
   Dying, and, behold, I live!

Thou, O Christ, Art all I want;
   More than all in Thee I find.
Raise the fallen, cheer the faint,
   Heal the sick, and lead the blind,
Just and holy is Thy name;
   I am all unrighteousness,
False and full of sin I am;
   Thou art full of truth and grace.

Plenteous grace with Thee is found,
   Grace to cover all my sin.
Let the healing streams abound
   Make and keep me pure within.
Thou of life the Fountain art,
   Freely let me take of Thee;
Spring Thou up within my heart,
   Rise to all eternity.

"A Mighty Fortress Is Our God"

God is our Refuge and Strength, a very present help in trouble. Therefore we will not fear though the earth should change, though the mountains shake in the heart of the sea; though its waters roar and foam, though the mountains tremble with its tumult. There is a river whose streams make glad the city of God, the holy habitation of the Most High. God is in the midst of her, she shall not be moved; God will help her right early. The nations rage, the kingdoms totter; He utters His voice, the earth melts. The Lord of hosts is with us; the God of Jacob is our refuge. Come, behold the works of the Lord, how He has wrought desolations in the earth. He makes wars cease to the end of the earth; He breaks the bow and shatters the spear, He burns the chariots with fire! "Be still, and know that I am God. I am exalted among the nations, I am exalted in the earth!" The Lord of hosts is with us; the God of Jacob is our Refuge.

Ps. 46 RSV

This psalm expresses the confidence of God's people. They rise above their human and earthly concerns to a firm faith in God's almighty power and His unchangeable grace and love in Jesus Christ. With God as their Savior and Defender they need not fear any evil. At all times and under all circumstances His presence and favor are their security, support and comfort. They know that their troubles are in God's hands and that He will make them turn out for their good, their peace, and their happiness.

The psalmist calls on all people to contemplate the wonders that God did for His people in the past and the destruction he brought about on His enemies. Therefore God calls on them to "be still" in humble submission and enduring faith. All should acknowledge Him and bow down to His universal, everlasting, and absolute rulership and love, if they would escape destruction and find deliverance, peace, and happiness for time and eternity. For all who have Christ as their Lord and Savior have the power, truth, and love of God as their "refuge and strength." In every danger, trial, and trouble they find him "a very present help." When Martin Luther received any discouraging news he used to say to his family and friends, "Come, let us sing the forty-sixth psalm."

In his book on Luther, *Here I Stand,* Roland H. Bainton tells us that "Luther felt that his depressions were necessary. At the same time they were dreadful and by all means and in every way to be avoided and overcome. This whole life was a struggle against them, and a fight for faith. This is the point at which he interests us so acutely, for we too are cast down and we too would know how to assuage our despondency."

He says that Luther had several methods to overcome depression. One was to meet the Devil head on. Luther described his bout with the Devil as follows:

"When I go to bed, the Devil is always waiting for me. When he begins to plague me, I give him this answer: 'Devil, I must sleep. That's God's command: Work by day. Sleep by night. So go away.' If that doesn't work and he brings out a catalog of sins, I say, 'Yes, old fellow, I know all about it. And I know some more you have overlooked. Here are a few extra. Put them down.' If he still won't quit and presses me hard and accuses me as a sinner, I scorn him and say, 'St. Satan, pray for me. Of course you have never done anything wrong in your life. You alone are holy. Go to God and get grace for yourself. If you want to get me all straightened out, I say, Physician, heal thyself.' "

"But always and above all else the one great objective aid for Luther was the Scripture, because this is the written record of the revelation of God in Christ. . . . What wonder then that Luther, in the years of his deepest depressions composed these lines: A mighty bulwark is our God."

The Holy Scriptures and the Sacraments are also our greatest aid for overcoming our depressions, fears, and troubles in our old age. When we experience the loss of loved ones, loneliness, inabilities, sickness, and the fear of death, let us say, "Come, let us sing the forty-sixth psalm." Let us pray for the increase of our faith. Then we have nothing to worry about. Our faith and patience will sometimes be tried; yet God will utter His voice and we shall triumph in peace. Let us pray for that glorious day when all evil will be gone and in reverent submission worship and trust our almighty Savior. Through life and death we shall then overcome every fear, depression, and concern with the confident cry, "The Lord of hosts is with us; the God of Jacob is our Refuge."

A mighty Fortress is our God,
   A trusty Shield and Weapon;
He helps us free from every need
   That hath us now o'ertaken.
The old evil Foe
Now means deadly woe;
Deep guile and great might
Are his dread arms in fight;
   On earth is not his equal.

With might of ours can naught be done,
   Soon were our loss effected;
But for us fights the Valiant One,
   Whom God Himself elected.
Ask ye, Who is this?
Jesus Christ it is,
Of Sabbeoth Lord,
And there's none other God;
   He holds the field forever.

Though devils all the world should fill,
   All eager to devour us,
We tremble not, we fear no ill,
   They shall not overpower us.
This world's prince may still
Scowl fierce as he will,
He can harm us none,
He's judged; the deed is done;
   One little word can fell him.

The Word they still shall let remain
   Nor any thanks have for it;

He's by our side upon the plain
  With His good gifts and Spirit.
And take they or life,
Goods, fame, child, and wife,
Let these all be gone,
They yet have nothing won;
  The Kingdom ours remaineth.

"Heaven Is My Home"

After this I looked, and behold, a great multitude which no man could number, from every nation, from all tribes and peoples and tongues, standing before the throne and before the Lamb, clothed in white robes, with palm branches in their hands, and crying with a loud voice, "Salvation belongs to our God, who sits upon the throne, and to the Lamb!" And all the angels stood round the throne and round the elders and the four living creatures, and they fell on their faces before the throne and worshiped God, saying, "Amen! Blessing and glory and wisdom and thanksgiving and honor and power and might be to our God for ever and ever! Amen."

Rev. 7:9-12 RSV

The problems of death and the concern about the life after death bother everyone. The elderly are especially concerned about these matters, because they know that they may not have much longer to live. Therefore it is important to consider the great questions about death and the hereafter. It is also impossible to have peace, hope, and happiness without a sure answer to these questions. Human beings have created and advocated many philosophical and religious theories about death and heaven. But these are only speculations. There is, however, a revelation directly from God our Creator and Redeemer, who alone can give us a sure and reliable knowledge about these things. This information is contained in the Holy Scriptures in words such as those in our text. It is also confirmed historically by our Lord Jesus Christ. He "came down from heaven," (John 6:41), died, and arose again. No one has ever done this. Therefore we can stake our life on Him and His word for our salvation and our future life.

In the Book of Revelation we have a description in picture language of heaven and the eternal glory and happiness that will be ours who believe in Christ and live according to His word. The glorified people who are in heaven are described as clothed in white robes and as having palm branches in their hands. White is the emblem of purity and righteousness. The persons in heaven were not by nature righteous and pure, but they were made pure and holy by the grace of God through faith in our Savior, Jesus Christ. Palm branches are an emblem of victory, peace, and joy. The people in heaven rejoice over peace between God and the world, which God established when He gave His Son to gain the victory over sin, death, and the devil by Christ's suffering, death, and glorious resurrection for our redemption. Through faith in Him that victory is ours, and we shall enjoy it for ever when we are in heaven. That is why the saints in heaven cry out with a loud voice, "Salvation belongs to our God, who sits upon the throne and worship God, saying, "Amen! Blessing and glory and wisdom and thanksgiving and honor and power and might be to our God for ever and ever! Amen."

After reading these things a certain person wrote, "We thus see what is the work of heaven, and we ought to begin it now, to get our hearts tuned to it, to be much in it, and to long for that world where our peace, as well as our happiness will be perfected." By being faithful unto death, we will be with the "great multitude which no man could number, from every nation, from all tribes and peoples and tongues, standing before the throne and before the Lamb, clothed in white robes, with palm branches in their hands."

Life is happy when there is something to live for, not for this world only but for an ultimate world of perfect, everlasting happiness and blessedness. We shall never find perfect happiness here. This life is full of jealousy, hatred, disappointment, sickness, pain, frustration, evil, and death. But we have something for which to live and to enable us to be happy now. With St. Paul we can say, "I consider that the sufferings of this present time are not worth comparing with the glory that is to be revealed to us" (Rom. 8:18 RSV). Let us live confidently and happily one day at a time, looking forward to our heavenly home. We shall then finally depart from this world in dignity and spend eternity in the blissful presence of God in heaven.

Hark! the sound of holy voices
　Chanting at the crystal sea,
Alleluia, Alleluia,
　Alleluia, Lord to Thee.
Multitudes which none can number
　Like the stars in glory stand,
Clothed in white apparel, holding
　Palms of victory in their hand.

Patriarchs and holy prophets,
　Who prepared the way of Christ,
King, apostle, saint, confessor,
　Martyr, and evangelist,
Saintly maiden, godly matron,
　Widows who have watched to prayer,
Joined in holy concert singing
　To the Lord of all, are there.

They have come from tribulation
　And have washed their robes in blood,
Washed them in the blood of Jesus;
　Tried they were, and firm they stood.
Mocked, imprisoned, stoned, tormented,
　Sawn asunder, slain with sword,
They have conquered death and Satan
　By the might of Christ the Lord.

Marching with Thy cross their banner,
　They have triumphed, following
Thee, the Captain of salvation,
　Thee, their Savior and their King.
Gladly, Lord, with Thee they suffered,
　Gladly, Lord, with Thee they died,
And by death to life immortal
　They were born and glorified.

Now they reign in heavenly glory,
　Now they walk in golden light,
Now they drink, as from a river,
　Holy bliss and infinite.
Love and peace they taste forever
　And all truth and knowledge see

54

In the beatific vision
  Of the blessed Trinity.
God of God, the One-begotten,
  Light of Light, Emmanuel,
In whose body, joined together,
  All the saints forever dwell,
Pour upon us of Thy fullness
  That we may forevermore
God the Father, God the Spirit,
  One with Thee on high, adore.

"God Is Love"

We know and believe the love God has for us. God is love, and he who abides in love abides in God, and God abides in him. In this is love perfected with us, that we may have confidence for the day of judgment, because as He is so are we in this world. There is no fear in love, but perfect love casts out fear. For fear has to do with punishment, and he who fears is not perfected in love. We love, because He first loved us.

1 John 4:16-19 RSV

"God is love." What a blessing it is to hear in our old age that God is love. But many do not subscribe to this statement. They say with a sneer, "If God were love, would He allow us to suffer terrible catastrophies, wars, epidemics, the destruction of properties and lives by fire, storms, floods, earthquakes, droughts, and depressions? Would He bring misery, unhappiness, pain, and sorrow to millions of people?" These arguments are not valid. No one will say that parents do not love their children when they punish them for wrongdoing. Why then should we say that God does not love us when He corrects us for our good in time and for eternity?

The fact is that God is love. The proof of this is seen already in the blessings we have in nature, in the talents He has given us, in the sciences, the arts, and the technologies we enjoy. But our text does not argue these questions. It simply tells us that God is love. The greatest proof of this is stated in these words: "God so loved the world that He gave his only Son, that whoever believes in Him should not perish but have eternal life" (John 3:16 RSV). When we believe in Christ and live in love we "have confidence for the day of judgment. . . . There is no fear in love, but perfect love casts out fear. For fear has to do with punishment."

The great historical fact of our redemption through Christ gives us comfort. It comforts us against our sins and a guilty conscience. It also strengthens and cheers us when we face problems and difficulties. We all have these, especially in old age. As we face these problems, let us remember that "God is love, and he who abides in love abides in God, and God abides in him." God loves us all, but the aged, the weary, the sick, the sorrowful, the wounded, the suffering—they lie nearest to the loving heart of God.

If we love and trust in God above all things, we will not fear. "There is no fear in love." "Fear not," the Bible says about 300 times.

> "Fear not, I am with you, oh, be not dismayed;
> For I am your God, and will still give you aid;
> I'll strengthen you, help you, and cause you to stand,
> Upheld by my righteous, omnipotent hand."

The love of God made little David the victor over the giant Goliath. It made Luther, a poor monk, face the temporal powers of the world and say, "Here I stand; I cannot do otherwise; God help me. Amen." Let us then pray without ceasing that we may more fully love Him who first loved us. Let us show our gratitude by being cheerful and confident in the love of God and the hope of eternal life. For God has revealed to us His love in Christ. He has declared to us the great salvation. He regenerated us by His Holy Spirit into a state of acceptance and the certainty of life with Him now and for ever. "Who shall separate us from the love of Christ? Shall tribulation, or distress, or persecution, or famine, or nakedness, or peril, or sword? . . . No, in all these things we are more than conquerors through Him who loved us. For I am sure that neither death, nor life, nor angels, nor principalities, nor things present, nor things to come, nor powers, nor height, nor depth, nor anything else in all creation will be able to separate us from the love of God in Christ Jesus our Lord" (Rom. 8:35-39 RSV).

O Love, who madest me to wear
    The image of Thy Godhead here;
Who soughtest me with tender care
    Through all my wanderings wild and drear—
O love, I give myself to Thee,
Thine ever, only Thine, to be.

O Love, who ere life's earliest dawn
    On me Thy choice hast gently laid;
O Love, who here as man wast born
    And like to us in all things made—
O Love, I give myself to Thee,
Thine ever, only Thine, to be.

O Love, who once in time wast slain
    Pierced through and through with bitter woe;
O Love, who wrestling thus, didst gain
    That we eternal joy might know—
O Love, I give myself to Thee,
Thine ever, only Thine, to be.

O Love, who thus hast bound me fast
    Beneath that easy yoke of Thine;
Love, who hast conquered me at last,
    Enrapturing this heart of mine—
O Love, I give myself to Thee,
Thine ever, only Thine, to be.

O Love, who lovest me for aye,
    Who for my soul dost ever plead;
O Love, who didst my ransom pay,
    Whose power sufficeth in my stead—
O Love, I give myself to Thee,
Thine ever, only Thine, to be.

O Love, who once shalt bid me rise
    From out this dying life of ours;
O Love, who once above yon skies
    Shalt set me in the fadeless bowers—
O Love, I give myself to Thee,
Thine ever, only Thine, to be.

"Jesus Sinners Does Receive"

Have mercy on me, O God, according to Thy steadfast love, according to Thy abundant mercy blot out my transgressions. Wash me thoroughly from my iniquity, and cleanse me from my sin!

Ps. 51:1-2 RSV

Now the tax collectors and sinners were all drawing near to hear Him. And the Pharisees and the scribes murmured, saying, "This man receives sinners and eats with them." So He told them this parable: "What man of you, having a hundred sheep, if he has lost one of them, does not leave the ninety-nine in the wilderness, and go after the one which is lost, until he finds it? And when he has found it, he lays it on his shoulders, rejoicing. And when he comes home, he calls together his friends and his neighbors, saying to them, 'Rejoice with me, for I have found my sheep which was lost.' Just so, I tell you, there will be more joy in heaven over one sinner who repents than over ninety-nine righteous persons who need no repentance."

Luke 15:1-7 RSV

Luther was brought up to think of Christ as a righteous, holy, and stern judge whom he had to placate with good works, self-punishment, and religious exercises in order to receive forgiveness of his sins. Groaning under sin and seeking deliverance by works of the Law he entered the Augustinian convent at Erfurt. But all his efforts proved in vain. Finally, through his study of the Holy Scriptures, he discovered that the all-terrible God is also the all-merciful God, for "God so loved the world that He gave His only Son, that whoever believes in Him should not perish but have eternal life" (John 3:16 RSV), and "A man is justified by faith apart from works of the Law" (Rom. 3:28 RSV). Then Luther found a gracious God in Christ, and so can we senior citizens.

In Psalm 51 the psalmist implores the mercy of God, his "steadfast love," his "abundant mercy." He does not mention his former good works, his good life, but as a miserable sinner, he dwells on the only cheering thought, namely that God would forgive his sins through the redemptive grace of the promised Savior.

Let us look at this parable carefully. It illustrates the fact that "Jesus sinners does receive." The more we study it, the more we shall love it. What a picture of all of us. We did not intend to get lost. We only followed our sinful human nature, temptations, and questionable desires and pleasures. But by the grace of God we finally discovered ourselves lost. Do we realize how much we mean to God? Think of the price He paid for our redemption. Christ redeemed us, as Luther's explanation of the Second Article says, "not with gold or silver, but with His holy, precious blood and with His innocent suffering and death." Let us ponder this fact and this parable. We become blue sometimes—discouraged, doubtful, and afraid. We feel guilty, lonely, useless, and hopeless. We think that no one cares. Well, if no one cares, even if we do not care very much about ourselves, God still cares. God still loves us. He is the ever-loving, concerned, seeking God.

To have a gracious, loving God is the greatest blessing. The world imagines that riches, honor, and ease constitute happiness. But all these things pass away and often end in a bad conscience and an unhappy death.

When we examine our conscience, let us confess our sins and pray that God may forgive them for Christ's sake. Let us take comfort in our gracious God and Shepherd. When the shepherd in the parable came home, he called together his friends and his neighbors, saying to them, "Rejoice with me, for I have found my sheep which was lost." "Just so, I tell you, there will be more joy in heaven over one sinner who repents than over ninety-nine righteous persons who need no repentance."

Let us look forward to the joy of heaven. It is the greatest, the deepest, the most perfect, the most enduring joy and happiness there is. "To Him who loves us and has freed us from our sins by His blood . . . to Him be glory and dominion for ever and ever. Amen" (Rev. 1:5-6 RSV).

Jesus sinners does receive;
  Oh, may all this saying ponder
Who in sin's delusions live
  And from God and heaven wander!
Here is hope for all who grieve—
Jesus sinners does receive.

We deserve but grief and shame,
  Yet His words, rich grace revealing,
Pardon, peace, and life proclaim.
  Here their ills have perfect healing
Who with humble hearts believe—
Jesus sinners does receive.

Sheep that from the fold did stray
  No true shepherd e'er forsaketh;
Weary souls that lost their way
  Christ, the Shepherd, gently taketh
In His arms that they may live—
Jesus sinners does receive.

Come, you sinners, one and all
  Come, accept His invitation;
Come, obey His gracious call,
  Come and take His free salvation!
Firmly in these words believe:
Jesus sinners does receive.

Oh, how blest it is to know:
  Were as scarlet my transgression,
It shall be as white as snow
  By Thy blood and bitter Passion;
For these words I now believe:
Jesus sinners does receive.

Jesus sinners does receive.
  Also I have been forgiven;
And when I this earth must leave,
  I shall find an open heaven.
Dying, still to Him I cleave—
Jesus sinners does receive.

Remember Your Baptism

It is better to suffer for doing right, if that should be God's will, than for doing wrong. For Christ also died for sins once for all, the righteous for the unrighteous, that He might bring us to God, being put to death in the flesh but made alive in the spirit; in which He went and preached to the spirits in prison, who formerly did not obey, when God's patience waited in the days of Noah, during the building of the ark, in which a few, that is, eight persons, were saved through water. Baptism, which corresponds to this, now saves you, not as a removal of dirt from the body but as an appeal to God for a clear conscience, through the resurrection of Jesus Christ, who has gone into heaven and is at the right hand of God, with angels, authorities, and powers subject to Him.

1 Peter 3:17-22 RSV

It is natural for us to rebel against suffering. That is also true in old age. It is then especially that we need the comfort and assurance that our baptism provides for us. Most of us were baptized as infants and we have no remembrance of it. But it has had an effect in us, and its benefits and blessings are ours throughout life. For in Holy Baptism we were made a child of God as our gracious and loving Father in Christ. To have God as our dear Father is the greatest comfort and assurance that anyone can have in his old age. For God is almighty. With Him nothing is impossible. God is faithful. He will never let us down. God is wise. He knows what is best for us. God is kind and loves His children. He has compassion on us also in our afflictions of old age.

In our text God reminds us through St. Peter that Christ died for our sins once and for all. He redeemed us from sin, death, and damnation. He is our Savior now and forever. St. Peter also reminds us of the days of Noah, when, through Noah, the Spirit of Christ preached repentance. At that time Noah's family, eight persons, were saved from the deadly flood through the ark. That flood was a picture of baptism. The destroying water was a symbol of the evil in us and the world.

The ark was a symbol of the holy Christian church. Noah and his family were saved in the ark. In Holy Baptism we entered, as it were, the ark. We became members of Christ's body, the church. As long as we are members of His body nothing can really harm us. We are in a state of grace. We are baptized. God has made an agreement with us. We can say every day, "The Lord is my Shepherd, I shall not want" (Ps. 23:1). A fellow Christian once told this writer that whenever he got into his car to drive on the bloody Bay-Shore highway, he would bless himself with the sign of the cross, with which he was signed in Holy Baptism, and say, "I was baptized; I am a dear child of God; His angels are with me; nothing can really harm me."

In the morning when we get up let us say, "I am baptized; I have the assurance of God: 'When I awake, I am still with Thee' (Ps. 139:18)." Let us start the day with the remembrance of our baptism. Let us repeat the words of our text, "It is better to suffer for doing right, if that should be God's will, than for doing wrong." During the day, let us keep busy with whatever we are able to do and commit all our troubles into the hands of our almighty, gracious, and loving Father. That will keep us from worry, fear, and self-pity. At night let us spend some time reading the Word of God and saying our evening prayers. Before going to sleep, let us thank God for everything and everyone, counting our blessings and naming them one by one. This will do away with all complaints. It will overcome all our discouragements. Then let us remember our baptism and commit our body and soul and all that we are and have into the keeping of God, saying to Him, "Into Your hands I commit myself. Let Your holy angels be with me that the evil foe may have no power over me. Be still, my soul. The longest night shall end. God's dawn the clouds shall rend, and brighter shine the perfect day."

The older we become, the more let us think of our baptismal grace. It is our greatest solace for time and eternity.

Baptized into Thy name most holy,
  O Father, Son, and Holy Ghost,
I claim a place, though weak and lowly,
  Among Thy seed, Thy chosen host.
Buried with Christ and dead to sin,
Thy Spirit now shall live within.

My loving Father, Thou dost take me
  To be henceforth Thy child and heir;
My faithful Savior, Thou dost make me
  The fruit of all Thy sorrows share;
Thou Holy Ghost, wilt comfort me
When darkest clouds around I see.

And I have vowed to fear and love Thee
  And to obey Thee, Lord, alone;
Because the Holy Ghost did move me
  I dared to pledge myself Thine own,
Renouncing sin to keep the faith
And war with evil unto death.

My faithful God, Thou failest never,
  Thy covenant surely will abide;
Oh, cast me not away forever
  Should I transgress it on my side!
Though I have oft my soul defiled,
Do Thou forgive, restore, Thy child.

Yea, all I am and love most dearly
  I offer now, O Lord, to Thee,
Oh, let me make my vows sincerely
  And help me Thine own child to be!
Let naught within me, naught I own,
Serve any will but Thine alone.

And never let my purpose falter,
  O Father, Son, and Holy Ghost,
But keep me faithful to Thine altar
  Till Thou shalt call me from my post.
So unto Thee I live and die
And praise Thee evermore on high.

"Rest for Your Soul"

At that time Jesus declared, "I thank Thee, Father, Lord of heaven and earth, that Thou hast hidden these things from the wise and understanding and revealed them to babes; yea, Father, for such was Thy gracious will. All things have been delivered to Me by My Father; and no one knows the Son except the Father, and no one knows the Father except the Son and any one to whom the Son chooses to reveal Him. Come to Me, all who labor and are heavy laden, and I will give you rest. Take My yoke upon you, and learn from Me; for I am gentle and lowly in heart, and you will find rest for your soul. For My yoke is easy, and My burden is light."

Matt. 11:25-30 RSV

Luther once suggested that every Christian should memorize this text in order to comfort himself in every cross, affliction, and difficulty, with the assurance that we have a Lord who gives us a right knowledge of God The text is full of consolation, for here Christ is pictured as He was once painted by Hoffmann, standing with hands outstretched and saying, "Come to me, all who labor and are heavy laden, and I will give you rest," or as Thorwaldsen likewise showed him in the statue called, "Come unto Me."

This is a sweet text for us especially in our old age. Christ describes God as Lord of heaven and earth in contrast to the worldly-wise and understanding. But though He is greater than anyone else, He has revealed Himself to his "babes," His children, to whom He is the great Father. Only those who are spiritually babes can receive Him, for these despair of their own wisdom and strength to gain salvation. But this Gospel invitation, "Come to Me, all who labor and are heavy laden," touches and moves their hearts to come and take.

What does our Lord mean when He promises us rest? Rest is a wonderful thing. How often we have looked forward to a time of rest! We have longed for it and hoped for it. So often we are weary in body, mind, and spirit. But the rest

Christ speaks of here is not primarily bodily rest. It is rest of the mind, the conscience, the soul. In old age we experience much physical unrest. Our bodies are not as strong as they used to be. We suffer from infirmities and sickness. Our hands tremble. Our nerves are tense. Our bodies are wrinkled and full of pain. But worse than bodily burdens are those of the mind, the conscience, and soul. Our wrongdoings, our sins, condemn us. We try to comfort ourselves with our good works. But are they good enough? Can they atone for our sins? Our conscience still accuses us and gives us no rest.

Then our Lord Jesus comes to us and says, "I will give you rest." This promise is based on who He is and what He has done for us. He is the Son of God who became one of us to redeem us from sin, death, and damnation. He suffered and died for us. He rose from death and triumphed for us over sin, Satan, and death. He tells us that when we believe in Him, when we trust in His atoning work for us, we shall not perish but have forgiveness, life, and salvation. In that way He gives us rest, rest of soul, mind, and body, too.

But there is one more thing that Christ tells us to do, which is also the gift of the Holy Spirit, as is faith in Christ. He says, "Take My Yoke upon you, and learn from me; for I am gentle and lowly in heart, and you will find rest for your soul. For My yoke is easy and My burden is light." A yoke is a piece of harness. It is a symbol of hard work. But let us not be afraid of this yoke, for it is Christ's yoke, He assumed it for us. Therefore it is easy and light. His yoke is love, meekness, and lowliness. It is a blessed yoke. It is the blessed fruit of His love. After we have come to Him, we are to be active in love. St. Bernard said, "What can be lighter than a burden that unburdens us, and a yoke that bears its bearer?" Luther said, "Christ's burden does not oppress, but makes light, and itself bears rather than is borne." Even when old age, afflictions, crosses, and many other trials are included, this yoke is easy and this burden is light. For it is filled with the greatest comfort and hope. It upholds us when all other comforts fail.

"Come unto Me, ye weary,
  And I will give you rest."
O blessed voice of Jesus,
  Which comes to hearts opprest!
It tells of benediction,
  Of pardon, grace, and peace,
Of joy that hath no ending,
  Of love which cannot cease.

"Come unto Me, ye wand'rers,
  And I will give you light."
O loving voice of Jesus,
  Which comes to cheer the night!
Our hearts were filled with sadness,
  And we had lost our way;
But Thou hast brought us gladness
  And songs at break of day.

"Come unto Me, ye fainting,
  And I will give you life."
O cheering voice of Jesus,
  Which comes to aid our strife!
The Foe is stern and eager,
  The fight is fierce and long;
But Thou has made us mighty
  And stronger than the strong.

"And whosoever cometh,
  I will not cast him out."
O patient love of Jesus,
  Which drives away our doubt,
Which, though we be unworthy
  Of love so great and free,
Invites us very sinners
  To come, dear Lord, to Thee!

Strength in Weakness

A thorn was given me in the flesh, a messenger of Satan, to harass me, to keep me from being too elated. Three times I besought the Lord about this, that it should leave me; but He said to me, "My grace is sufficient for you, for My power is made perfect in weakness." I will all the more gladly boast of my weakness, that the power of Christ may rest upon me. For the sake of Christ, then, I am content with weakness, insults, hardships, persecutions and calamities; for when I am weak, then I am strong.

2 Cor. 12:7-10 RSV

St. Paul was a highly gifted and sincere Christian man. He was called to be a missionary and went from country to country preaching the Gospel. Unselfishly he devoted himself to this work, suffering great hardships and persecution for the sake of the salvation of his fellow persons everywhere. But he was not to forget that he was feeble and sinful, entirely dependent on the grace and mercy of God. Therefore God allowed him to suffer bodily infirmities of a distressing nature. He says, "A thorn was given me in the flesh, a messenger of Satan, to harass me, to keep me from being too elated." What this was particularly we are not told. But whatever it was, it was a great and distressing burden, and in his suffering he besought the Lord three times that it should leave him. But the Lord did not grant his request, since He knew that this trial was good for him, and He wished to illustrate the power of His grace. Therefore St. Paul was satisfied to continue his work under this affliction. At the same time the Lord assured him that His grace was sufficient for him and that He would support and comfort him in his affliction. Then St. Paul's mind was composed. Yes, with heartfelt joy he said, "I will all the more gladly boast of my weakness, that the power of Christ may rest upon me." He found that through his weakness he was actually made strong.

Whatever there is in our experience as senior citizens, whether outward trials or inward conflicts, we may consider these as a thorn in the flesh that God permits in His wisdom and love for our welfare and benefit now and forever. God knows what is best for us. Let us remember this when Satan would fill us with doubt, fear, and unbelief. Let us not do what Satan wants us to do, namely think that we have lost faith and that God has given us over to perdition. That is not the case. From St. Paul's example we see that God permits His saints to be afflicted in order to keep them humble. He wants to remind them of their utter helplessness apart from His grace and protecting power.

When we are afflicted with sickness and other troubles, let us pray earnestly and confidently. Christ is our "merciful and faithful high priest" (Heb. 2:17). "Because He himself has suffered and been tempted, He is able to help those who are tempted" (Heb. 2:18 RSV). Then if the desired deliverance is delayed, let us not be discouraged. He often answers our prayers by increasing our strength for the conflict we face in our old age. Sometimes He gives us such views of His grace that we can most gladly boast of our weakness, as St. Paul did in his afflictions. The power of Christ will rest upon us and will enable us even to take pleasure in our infirmities. We must trust in God's wisdom as well as His truth and not be discouraged. When we strive against sin, bear up under discouragement, and depend on Him, we may be sure that His grace is sufficient for us and His power is made perfect in weakness.

When Satan attacks us, let us do as Martin Luther did. He said, "Once the devil told me, 'Martin Luther, you are a great sinner and you will be damned.' 'Stop! Stop!' said I; One thing at a time. I am a great sinner, that is true, I confess it. What next?' 'Therefore you will be damned.' 'That is not good reasoning. It is true, I am a great sinner, but it is written that

70

Jesus Christ came to save sinners; therefore I shall be saved! now go your way!' So I cut the devil off with his own sword, and he went away mourning because he could not cast me down by calling me a sinner."

Commit thou all thy griefs
  And ways into His hands,
To His sure truth and tender care
  Who earth and heaven commands.

No profit canst thou gain
  By self-consuming care;
To Him commend thy cause; His ear
  Attends the softest prayer.

Thy everlasting truth,
  Father, Thy ceaseless love,
Sees all Thy children's wants and knows
  What best for each will prove.

Through waves and clouds and storms
  He gently clears thy way;
Wait thou His time; so shall this night
  Soon end in joyous day.

Thou seest our weakness, Lord;
  Our hearts are known to Thee;
Oh, lift Thou up the sinking hand,
  Confirm the feeble knee!

Let us, in life, in death,
  Thy steadfast truth declare
And publish with our latest breath
  Thy love and guardian care.

"Looking to Jesus"

Now faith is the assurance of things hoped for, the conviction of things not seen. For by it the men of old received divine approval.
Heb. 11:1-2 RSV

In Hebrews 11 the apostle defines faith and gives examples of great men of faith, such as Abel, Enoch, Moses, and David. This "cloud of witnesses" (Heb. 12:1 RSV) is an object lesson for us. Faith in Jesus Christ overcomes persecutions and gives patience, endurance, and victory.

We should consider ourselves surrounded by these and other witnesses of the Christian faith. They are a powerful testimony of God's grace and loving kindness. These persons and many others are, as it were, looking down from heaven on us, supporting our cause in the difficulties, dangers, and concerns we experience. For they themselves have run the race and have gained the great victory.

"Let us also lay aside every weight, and sin which clings so closely," (Heb. 12:1 RSV) and not burden ourselves with worldly cares that hinder our spiritual progress and endanger the winning of our race. Let us watch against natural sinful thoughts and deeds that continually "cling so closely," and take advantage of every opportunity to win the race.

We should especially use the means of grace God has given us to sustain and strengthen our faith—His Word and the sacrament of Holy Communion. This will enable us to overcome unbelief, the love of the world, and the fear of suffering. By these means God will enable us to "run with perseverance" and to "look to Jesus, the pioneer and perfecter" of our faith (Heb. 12:1-2 RSV).

We must look to Christ, "who for the joy that was set before Him endured the cross, despising the shame, and is seated at the right hand of the throne of God" (Heb. 12:2

RSV). From Him comes our salvation. He alone produces faith by the Holy Spirit and keeps us in the true faith unto the end. He gives us patience and endurance. His example of love and suffering for us and His example of meekness cannot fail to lift up our drooping spirits with an assurance of His tender concern for our welfare.

We shall then see the "joy that was set before Him" (Heb. 12:2 RSV) and the joy that is ours through faith in Him. His Word, support, and power will comfort us under all circumstances. What are our sufferings compared to those of many others in different ages and places? We have "not yet resisted unto blood" (Heb. 12:4 KJV), as many others have done. Compared to them we have very little reason to complain.

"Looking to Jesus" (Heb. 12:2 RSV). Surely you have seen a mother looking at her baby. How intense that look! This is how we should look to our Lord Jesus. Perhaps you have seen an artist looking at a picture of a great master. He studies every feature. He looks at it patiently and long. He looks not merely to admire it but to imitate it. Probably you have seen a pilot looking at the guiding light in a harbor when the night was pitch black and the wind blowing hard. He knows that his safety depends on steering to that light. So let us look to Jesus, our Light and Savior.

Once during the war between the Spanish and the French, the Spanish sent a note to the French commander, General Coligny: "Surrender! We are more numerous than you." Then General Coligny wrote his reply on a piece of paper and fastened it to an arrow and shot it into the Spanish camp. The note said, "Surrender? Never! We have a Savior and King with us." Likewise when we are tempted to give up because of the troubles and suffering of old age, the loneliness and helplessness, we can fling back the defiant answer, "We have a Savior and King with us!"

In all circumstances and at all times, let us keep our eyes on our Lord Jesus. The more we look to Him in everything, the greater our peace, hope, and happiness. When difficulties are to be faced and clouds obscure our eyes, let us look up to our Savior. He never fails us. At the same time, let us never forget the hosts of the faithful who are the unseen spectators of our troubles and conquests. Looking to Jesus and remaining true and faithful, we shall find comfort and happiness now, and, in the end, the crown of glory.

For all the saints who from their labors rest,
Who Thee by faith before the world confest,
Thy name, O Jesus, be forever blest.
Alleluia! Alleluia!

Thou wast their Rock, their Fortress, and their Might;
Thou, Lord, their Captain in the well-fought fight;
Thou, in the darkness drear, their one true Light.
Alleluia! Alleluia!

Oh, may Thy soldiers faithful, true, and bold,
Fight as the saints who nobly fought of old
And win with them the victor's crown of gold.
Alleluia! Alleluia!

O blest communion, fellowship divine,
We feebly struggle, they in glory shine;
Yet all are one in Thee, for all are Thine.
Alleluia! Alleluia!

The golden evening brightens in the west;
Soon, soon, to faithful warriors cometh rest.
Sweet is the calm of Paradise the blest.
Alleluia! Alleluia!

From earth's wide bounds, from ocean's farthest coast,
Through gates of pearl streams in the countless host,
Singing to Father, Son, and Holy Ghost,
Alleluia! Alleluia!

Why Worry?

Do not be anxious, saying, "What shall we eat?" or "What shall we drink?" or "What shall we wear?" For the Gentiles seek all these things; and your heavenly Father knows that you need them all. But seek first His kingdom and His righteousness, and all these things shall be yours as well.

Matt. 6:31-33 RSV

Here our Lord speaks about worrying. Worry causes more unhappiness and destroys more people than all other ills to which our human flesh is heir. But we Christians are, or at least ought to be, without worry. Of course we should be concerned about our duties and problems. We should try to find the right way of doing things. We are to know ourselves. But we should not worry. Christ tells us that our heavenly Father knows all our needs. What is more, He can supply them. God is the great Householder of the universe. He opens His hands and satisfies the desire of every living thing. The birds of the air, which are so gay and cheerful, are provided with food and shelter. The lilies of the field "neither toil nor spin" (Matt. 6:28). Yet even Solomon in all his glory was not arrayed like one of these.

Luther, who was a good student of nature, estimated that the sparrows alone cost God more every year than the income of the richest man of his time, the king of France. Audubon, the great naturalist, estimated that the passenger pigeons in a single breeding place in Ohio needed 9 million bushels of food daily. Now think of the millions of birds in the world and consider how much they need every day. Yet "they neither sow nor reap nor gather into barns, yet your heavenly Father feeds them" (Matt. 6:26 RSV).

Just as wonderful is the lesson of the lilies. These examples should stop people from worrying. Of course, they cannot show a sinner the way to heaven. That is done only by the Word of God through the Holy Spirit, who brings us to faith in Christ and salvation. But when a person has become a Christian, the study of nature may help him from worrying.

It is true that sometimes it seems that God has forsaken us. But such thoughts are false. He never forsakes His children who trust in Him. For "as a father pities his children, so the Lord pities those who fear Him" (Ps. 103:13 RSV). As He is faithful to us, it is our duty to be faithful to Him—to live according to His will, to pray to Him, and to leave everything to Him with childlike faith, as dear children trust in their loving parents. Our heavenly Father knows what we need for the welfare of our bodies and souls. He will supply what we need. He will take care of us in all times, all places, all sicknesses, all troubles, all circumstances of old age, and whatever bothers us as senior citizens. He is our *heavenly* Father who is not limited in His ability to help. Put your trust in Him.

Suppose you were sent on a trip from San Francisco to Jerusalem, and before you started you were given certified bank checks to be cashed in the cities where you had to stop over on the way. These could be lost, stolen, or destroyed by fire. Then you would worry and say to yourself, "Suppose I get to London and my checks are gone; what will become of me? I'm afraid I will starve." That would be foolish, you say. But it is not half so foolish as to have the word of the almighty and loving God and then go fearing, cast down, and worried on life's journey. No fire, no thief can destroy the checks of God.

To worry is to doubt your heavenly Father's word, ability, love, and faithfulness. Let us not be guilty of such doubt, but let us thank Him and trust in Him who has fed and clothed us from the day we were born. "He who did not spare His own Son, but gave Him up for us all, will He not also give us all things with Him?" (Rom. 8:32 RSV). In view of the fact that Christ lived, died, and arose again for us and our salvation, shall we doubt and worry about the love and care of our heavenly Father? What He lets us experience is all designed for our good. If we trust in Him, it will all end in a happy issue. Therefore let us leave everything in God's hands. He will discipline us, but He will never let us down. He will never let us perish.

Do not measure God's love and favor by your feelings. The sun shines as clearly on the darkest day as on the brightest. The difference is not in the sun, but in the clouds that hinder the light of the sun. So God's love is as great when He does not shine in brightness as when He does. Job was as much loved by God in the midst of his miseries as he was later, when he came to enjoy the abundance of His mercies. Let us not worry. Let us trust the promises of God and daily look to His goodness to supply us with all we need now and forever. "His goodness all our day attends. His loving kindness never ends."

I leave all things to God's direction,
    He loveth me in weal and woe;
His will is good, true His affection,
    With tender love His heart doth glow.
My Fortress and my Rock is He.
What pleaseth God, that pleaseth me.
My God hath all things in His keeping,
    He is the ever faithful Friend;
He grants me laughter after weeping,
    And all His ways in blessings end.
His love endures eternally.
What pleaseth God, that pleaseth me.
God knows what must be done to save me,
    His love for me will never cease;
Upon His hands He did engrave me
    With purest gold of loving grace.
His will supreme must ever be!
What pleaseth God, that pleaseth me.
My God desires the soul's salvation,
    Me also He desires to save;
Therefore with Christian resignation
    All earthly troubles I will brave.
His will be done eternally.
What pleaseth God, that pleaseth me.

Hope and Happiness

Blessed be the God and Father of our Lord Jesus Christ! By His great mercy we have been born anew to a living hope through the resurrection of Jesus Christ from the dead, and to an inheritance which is imperishable, undefiled, and unfading, kept in heaven for you, who by God's power are guarded through faith for a salvation ready to be revealed in the last time. . . . As the outcome of your faith you obtain the salvation of your souls.

1 Peter 1:3-5, 9 RSV

As Christians "we have been born anew to a living hope." This hope is based on the fact that Christ has redeemed us from sin, Satan, and hell. Through faith in Christ we have forgiveness of our sins, a gracious and loving God, and the assurance of an inner life of blessedness, hope, and happiness now and forever.

The result of Christian faith is hope. Hope is called the anchor of the soul. What an anchor is to a ship that hope is to a Christian. It does not matter to a ship whether the storm drives or the current drifts or the rocks threaten it, if the anchor holds, all is well.

The Bible is full of promises that give hope. The trouble is that we do not read and study the Scriptures enough to get the comfort and hope that it contains. The apostle tells us that we who are by nature sinful and guilty, "dead through . . . trespasses and sin (and) children of wrath" [Eph. 2:1-3 RSV], God has "born anew to a living hope through the resurrection of Jesus Christ from the dead."

Non-Christians also have hope. They hope for earthly things, such as money, honor, social connections, parties, and good times. They hope in all kinds of idols. But these hopes give no real and lasting satisfaction. They deceive and finally end in a hopeless death.

But we Christians have "a living hope," and an

inheritance that is far different from that which worldly people look for and desire. Earthly hopes and inheritances are perishable both in themselves and in those who depend on them. But the hopes and inheritances of Christians are "imperishable, undefiled, and unfading." Christian hope is a firm assurance given us by the Holy Spirit through God's word and sacraments. St. Peter gives us a wonderful description of our Christian hope. He says that it is "imperishable, undefiled, unfading, kept in heaven for you." Those who have this hope are "guarded." "Guarded" is a military word. It means garrisoned. It is protected. It cannot be taken away by enemies. The almighty God gives it to us and protects it. It is sure as long as we do not reject it wilfully. But we do not yet have possession of it in full.

The road that leads to the full possession is sometimes steep and rough. As long as we are here on earth we suffer grief and many trials, especially in our old age. But these experiences are all for our good. We do not suffer them because God hates us. St. Peter tells us that they are a proof or a testing of our faith. They are a discipline to give us strength and to build us up, to make us better Christians. They are really a blessing. They lead us to a closer fellowship with Christ.

St. Peter says, "Though now for a little while you may have to suffer various trials, so that the genuineness of your faith, more precious than gold which though perishable is tested by fire, may redound to praise and glory and honor at the revelation of Jesus Christ" (1 Peter 1:6-7 RSV). Fire does not only discover what is true gold, but makes the true gold more pure. It comes out pure, because it is severed from soil and dross and is more in value. Joseph found his crucible in an Egyptian prison, but he came out a man of great character. Purity of character and a stronger faith and hope are often attained by various trials.

Remember the story of the pilgrim in Bunyan's *Pilgrim's Progress*. The Christian pilgrim went through the slough of despondency, great troubles, and discouragement. But finally as he climbed the delectable mountains, the old, wearisome burden fell from his back. He was a new person in a new world. This is a picture of our Christian life. We are the children of God. We are pilgrims on earth. But one of these days we shall reach our goal. We shall stand before God clothed in white robes and with the palm of victory in our hands. Then we shall sing with the saints in heaven, "Hallelujah! For the Lord our God the Almighty reigns. Let us rejoice and exult and give Him the glory" (Rev. 19:6-7 RSV). What a great fulfillment of our hope and happiness!

My hope is built on nothing less
Than Jesus' blood and righteousness;
I dare not trust the sweetest frame,
But wholly lean on Jesus' name.
On Christ, the solid Rock, I stand;
All other ground is sinking sand.

When darkness veils His lovely face,
I rest on His unchanging grace;
In every high and stormy gale
My anchor holds within the veil.
On Christ the solid Rock I stand;
All other ground is sinking sand.

His oath, His covenant, and blood
Support me in the whelming flood;
When every earthly prop gives way,
He then is all my Hope and Stay.
On Christ, the solid Rock, I stand;
All other ground is sinking sand.

When He shall come with trumpet sound,
Oh, may I then in Him be found,
Clothed in His righteousness alone,
Faultless to stand before the throne!
On Christ, the solid Rock I stand;
All other ground is sinking sand.

The Blessing of Having a
Christian Family

And the Lord restored the fortunes of Job, when he had prayed for his friends; and the Lord gave Job twice as much as he had before. Then came to him all his brothers and sisters and all who had known him before, and ate bread with him in his house; and they showed him sympathy and comforted him for all the evil that the Lord had brought upon him; and each of them gave him a piece of money and a ring of gold. And the Lord blessed the latter days of Job more than his beginning; and he had fourteen thousand sheep, six thousand camels, a thousand yoke of oxen, and a thousand she-asses. He also had seven sons and three daughters. And he called the name of the first Jemimah; and the name of the second Keziah; and the name of the third Kerenhappuch. And in all the land there were no women so fair as Job's daughters; and their father gave them inheritance among their brothers. And after this Job lived a hundred and forty years, and saw his sons, and his sons' sons, four generations. And Job died, an old man, and full of days.

Job 42:10-17 RSV

As soon as Job repented and submitted himself to God, his character was reestablished and made more illustrious than before. The permission given to Satan having been revoked, Job's health, children, friends, and prosperity were restored. After this he lived in honor and happiness 140 years. He saw his posterity to the fourth generation. After that he died in peace, thanking God for his blessings.

Instead of being discouraged and unhappy in our old age, let us think of the blessing that is ours for having raised a Christian and successful family. This blessing compensates for all the troubles and disabilities that come with old age. It is indeed very painful to be reduced to weakness, forced retirement, various sicknesses, and imminent death. But when we look at our blessings and submit to God's will, our self-confidence, peace, and happiness will be restored.

We should be careful not to judge anything before the time.

We do not know how the Lord will clear up our difficulties. Nor are we competent to judge who is the most happy person. For the end crowns the day. Satan's power over us is limited in ability as well as in degree. When he is rebuked, the adversity of those whom he has afflicted will be dispelled. Then the way of happiness will be restored. When we have stood the trial, we shall come forth as gold purified in the furnace of fire.

Whether the Lord gives us health, long life, affluence, friends, and flourishing families or not, we shall be happy eventually if we suffer patiently according to God's will. Those things which we thought were against us will in the end be our greatest and most enduring blessings. Having raised a devoted family and good children is a blessing for which we can be proud and thankful. Let us now think of this and be happy.

We do not know for what good purposes our lives are prolonged. Therefore let us not be impatient or discouraged. Whether our friends or children go before or follow us into eternity, they will not be lost to us if we have raised them as Christians. This above all is the greatest blessing. It is more valuable than all the wealth, honor, and personal accomplishments in other things.

Though Job's trials and their happy outcome are full of instruction and consolation for us, our greatest comfort and happiness is in looking to our Lord Jesus. His sufferings were vastly greater than those of Job. He endured them with perfect patience. They resulted in far greater glory. He was tempted and suffered for us. He triumphed and was glorified for us. For us He offered Himself as a sacrifice. For us He pleads before the throne of the heavenly Father. In Him we are pardoned and accepted. He sees His offspring, He prolongs his days, the will of the Lord prospers in His hand (Is. 53:10-11). To Him we must come. From Him we must receive all that we need. Let us then experience His grace, share in His victory, follow in His steps and copy His patience. "Therefore do not throw away your confidence, which has a great reward. For you have need of endurance, so that you may do the will of God and receive what is promised" (Heb. 10:35-36).

Oh, blest the house, whate'er befall,
Where Jesus Christ is all in all!
Yea, if He were not dwelling there,
How dark and poor and void it were!

Oh, blest the house where faith ye find
And all within have set their mind
To trust their God and serve Him still
And do in all His holy will!

Oh, blest the parents who give heed
Unto their children's foremost need
And weary not of care or cost!
May none to them and heaven be lost!

Blest such a house, it prospers well,
In peace and joy the parents dwell
And in their children's lot is shown
How richly God can bless His own.

Then here will I and mine today
A solemn covenant make and say:
Though all the world forsake Thy Word,
I and my house will serve the Lord.

Old Age

A long time afterward, when the Lord had given rest to Israel from all their enemies round about, and Joshua was old and well advanced in years, Joshua summoned all Israel, their elders and heads, their judges and officers, and said to them: "I am now old and well advanced in years; and you have seen all that the Lord your God has done to all the nations for your sake, for it is the Lord your God who has fought for you. And now I am about to go the way of all the earth, and you know in your hearts and souls, all of you, that not one thing has failed of all the good things which the Lord your God promised concerning you; all have come to pass for you, not one of them has failed."

Joshua 23:1-3, 14 RSV

God had made wonderful promises to the fathers of the children of Israel. These had all been fulfilled. The Israelites had been highly blessed, and Joshua was deeply moved by all that God had done for His people.

Now Joshua was "old and well advanced in years." He knew that his end was near. He "summoned all Israel" and said to them, "I am about to go the way of all the earth." With almost his last breath he reminded his people most solemnly that not one of the things had failed of all the good which the Lord their God had promised concerning them; all had come to pass for them, not one of them had failed.

As old people we need to use our wisdom, experience, and influence to extol God and to promote His Word and promises. We need to encourage everyone to practice what we have learned from the Holy Scriptures and from our experiences.

For ourselves, we need to meditate on the past and present grace and loving-kindness of God towards us. We need to reflect on His gracious promises in the Gospel of Christ and treasure the experiences we have had when God carried out His words faithfully. This will strengthen our faith and our expectation for the completion of these promises when He takes us out of this world.

At present God tells us, "Take good heed to yourselves . . . to love the Lord your God." Love and trust in Him, for we have many enemies. The most dangerous are the ones within ourselves, such as doubts, worries, fear, and despondency. These give us much trouble. Therefore we need to pray and make use of God's Word, the sacrament of Holy Communion, the service of our pastor, our hymnbook and other devotional literature published by the Christian church. The warfare with our enemies will require great courage and resolution on our part. But we need not fear our foes. For "it is the Lord your God who fights for you, as He promised you." Only "cleave to the Lord your God as you have done to this day." Then nothing will really harm us. We shall suffer sickness, pain, and death. Valuable friends may be removed. But God will not leave us or forsake us. He lives to protect, to uphold, to guide, to comfort, and to bless us. Let us trust in His Word and promises, His faithfulness, His love, and His power.

Joshua's courage was based on God's Word and promises. It was not a natural gift, but a gift of God's grace. At times his courage failed him. There were times when he wished that he had stayed on the other side of the Jordan River instead of crossing over to conquer the promised land. But in the hour of weakness he turned to God for help and renewed courage. That was the source of his strength, as it is ours, and the Lord did not let him down. When dangers and death seem too great for us, when courage fails us, let us turn to God for faith and strength. He will hear our prayers and give us the strength we need.

> Art thou weary, art thou troubled,
>   Art thou sore distressed?
> "Come to Me," saith One, "and, coming,
>   Be at rest."
>
> Hath He marks to lead me to Him,
>   If He be my Guide?
> "In his feet and hands are woundprints,
>   And His side."

Hath He diadem, as Monarch,
    That His brow adorns?
"Yea, a crown, in very surety,
    But of thorns."

If I find Him, if I follow,
    What His guerdon here?
"Many a sorrow, many a labor,
    Many a tear."

If I still hold closely to Him,
    What hath He at last?
"Sorrow vanquished, labor ended,
    Jordan passed."

If I ask Him to receive me,
    Will He say me nay?
"Not till earth and not till heaven
    Pass away."

Finding, following, keeping, struggling,
    Is He sure to bless?
"Saints, apostles, prophets, martyrs,
    Answer, Yes."

Selected Prayers

Morning Prayer

In the name of the Father and of the Son and of the Holy Spirit.

I thank You, my heavenly Father, through Jesus Christ, Your dear Son, that You have kept me this night from all harm and danger. Now I ask You to keep me this day also from sin and every evil, so that all my doings and life may please You. For into Your hands I commit myself, my body and soul, and all things. Let your holy angel be with me, in order that the wicked Foe may have no power over me. Amen.

Evening Prayer

In the name of the Father and of the Son and of the Holy Spirit.

I thank you, my heavenly Father, through Jesus Christ, Your dear Son, that You graciously kept me busy this day with things that I was able to do for my own good and for the welfare of others. Please forgive me all my sins and wrongdoings for Christ's sake, and graciously keep me this night. Into Your hands I commit myself, my body and soul, and all things. Let your holy angel be with me to protect and keep me from all harm and danger. If it be Your will, grant that I may go to sleep at once and sleep peacefully throughout the night, so that I may awake refreshed and happy in the morning. Amen.

Prayer Before Meals

(Say the Lord's Prayer and the following)

Lord God, heavenly Father, bless us and these Your gifts which we have received from Your bountiful goodness, through Jesus Christ, our Lord. Amen.

Prayer After Meals

Oh, give thanks unto the Lord, for He is good, for His mercy endures forever.

(Say the Lord's Prayer and the following)

We thank You, Lord God, heavenly Father, through Jesus Christ, our Lord, for the food we have received and for all other gifts and benefits, for all we are and have comes from You. Amen.

Strength for Daily Needs

O God, from whom I have received life and all earthly and spiritual blessings, grant me each day what I need. Help me to keep busy with something helpful to me and others as long as I am able to do some work. And when that is no longer possible, help me to pass my time in prayer and meditation of Your Word. Grant that I may always serve You and my fellow persons. Sanctify my good days and my days of trial, and give me grace to seek first Your kingdom and its righteousness, in the sure and certain faith that all else shall be added unto me; through Jesus Christ, Your Son, my Lord, who lives and reigns with You and the Holy Spirit, forever and ever. Amen.

For Protection

O Lord, give ear to my prayers and dispose the way of Your servant in safety under Your protection, that amid all the changes of my earthly pilgrimage, I may always be guarded by Your almighty aid; through Jesus Christ, my Lord, who lives and reigns with You and the Holy Spirit, forever and ever. Amen.

Thanksgiving

Heavenly Father, with thankful and humble heart I come to You. I thank You for all the benefits and blessings I have received from Your mercy and loving-kindness. It is to Your blessing that I owe what success I have had—every opportunity for doing good, every impulse for doing what is right, every victory I have gained over Satan and my sinful self. The best thanksgiving I can offer You is to live according to Your holy will. Grant me every day to do so more perfectly, and to grow in the knowledge of Your grace and love in Christ Jesus, my Lord and Savior, who lives and reigns with You and the Holy Spirit forever and ever. Amen.

For Heavenly-Mindedness

O merciful God, fill my heart with the graces of Your Holy Spirit, with love, joy, peace, longsuffering, gentleness, goodness, faith, meekness, temperance. Teach me to love those who hate me, to pray for those who despitefully use me, that I may be Your child. You are my heavenly Father. You make the sun to shine on the evil and the good and send rain on the just and on the unjust. In adversity grant me grace to be patient, in prosperity keep me humble, and at all times help me to guard my lips. Help me to esteem lightly the pleasures of this world and to thirst after heavenly things; through Jesus Christ, my Lord, who lives and reigns with You and the Holy Spirit, forever and ever. Amen.

In Loneliness

Lord Jesus, I beseech You by the loneliness of Your suffering on the cross, be near me in my loneliness, frustration, sorrow, and suffering. Let the comfort of Your presence transform my loneliness into comfort, consolation, and holy fellowship with You, for You have promised to be with me always, even unto death. You are my Lord and Savior, who lives and reigns with the Father and the Holy Spirit forever and ever. Amen.

In Sickness

Lord God, heavenly Father, it has pleased You to visit me with bodily infirmities. I know that You love me and will not permit anything to come upon me unless it is for my welfare and blessing. Grant that I may receive Your visitation and that my sickness may be to Your honor and glory and to my eternal salvation; through Jesus Christ, my Lord. Amen.

Repentance and Forgiveness

Dear God and Father, my days are in Your hands. Do with me as it pleases You. Only be gracious unto me for Christ's sake. You know all my sins. I am deeply sorry for these and repent of them. Please forgive me for the sake of Him who atoned for them with His holy, precious blood. Give me Your assurance through faith that You are gracious unto me and that at the end I will most certainly be saved; through the same Jesus Christ, my Lord. Amen.

For Peace

Almighty God, direct in peace my life, trustfully, fearlessly and, if it be Your will, painlessly. Take me when You want into the abode of Your chosen people without shame or stain or sin; for the sake of Jesus Christ, Your Son, my Lord, who lives and reigns with You and the Holy Spirit forever and ever. Amen.

In Sickness

"This slight momentary affliction is preparing for us an eternal weight of glory beyond all comparison, because we look not to the things that are seen but to the things that are unseen; for the things that are seen are transient, but the things that are unseen are eternal" (2 Cor. 4:17-18 RSV).

Almighty and everlasting God, the consolation of the

sorrowful and the strength of the weak, let my prayer in tribulation and my cry in distress come before You, so that I may see and receive Your promised help and comfort and deliverance; through Jesus Christ, my Lord. Amen.

For Forgiveness

O Almighty God, merciful Father, I a poor sinner confess unto You all my sins with which I have ever offended You and justly deserved Your temporal and eternal punishment. But I am heartily sorry for them and sincerely repent of them. Of your boundless mercy, and for the sake of the holy, innocent, bitter suffering and death of Your beloved Son, Jesus Christ, be gracious and merciful to me, a poor sinful being. Amen.

Preparation for Death

Almighty and everlasting God, dear, faithful heavenly Father, comfort me, strengthen me, spare me through Your great mercy. Help me out of all agony and distress. Release me in Your grace. Take me to Yourself into Your heavenly kingdom. Into Your hands I commit myself. You have redeemed me, O faithful God, through the death and resurrection of Jesus Christ, my Lord and Savior, who lives and reigns with You and the Holy Spirit forever and ever. Amen.

For Positive Desires

Grant me, O Holy Spirit, that whatever things are true, whatever things are honorable, whatever things are just, whatever things are pure, whatever things are lovely and of good reputation, whatever things are useful and beneficial— that I think about these things, thank You for them, and order my life according to them; through Jesus Christ Our Lord. Amen.

Trust in God

Lord God, heavenly Father, I praise You for ordering all things for my earthly and eternal good, and I ask You mercifully to enlighten my mind and give me a firm and continuing trust in Your loving care, so that rising above my afflictions and anxieties, I may rest on You, the Rock of everlasting Strength; through Jesus Christ Our Lord. Amen.

Trust in God's Help

My faithful God, once again I flee to You. I have no one besides You to whom I can turn in my distress. You know my troubles, and Your fatherly heart pities me. It may appear as though Your face is hidden from me, and Your mercy may seem to have an end. I confess that I am not deserving of Your help. And yet I am Your child, baptized into Your name, and saved by the blood of Jesus Christ. For His sake, have mercy upon me and help me. Strengthen me by Your Spirit, that I may patiently await the hour when it shall please You to deliver me from my distress; through Jesus Christ, Your Son, Our Lord. Amen.

Scripture Index